BE THE LEADER

You Were Meant to Be

LeRoy Eims

While this book is intended for the reader's
personal enjoyment and profit, it is also designed
for group study. A personal and group study guide
is located at the end of this text.

VICTOR BOOKS

A DIVISION OF SCRIPTURE PRESS PUBLICATIONS INC.
USA CANADA ENGLAND

Unless otherwise indicated, all Scripture quotations in this book are from the *Holy Bible, New International Version®*. Copyright © 1973, 1978, 1984 by International Bible Society. Used by permission of Zondervan Publishing House. All rights reserved, other quotations are from the *Authorized (King James) Version.*

Design: Scott Rattray
Cover Photo: Tony Stone Images: Steven Peters
Study Guide by: Susan Moroney

ISBN: 1-56476-573-x

27 28 29 30 31 32 33 34 35 36 Printing/Year 00 99 98 97 96

To Mrs. Dawson Trotman,
woman of God,
spiritual mother to thousands,
in every corner of the earth.

About the Author

LeRoy Eims is director of evangelism worldwide for The Navigators, an international organization training Christians to reproduce in others their life-changing relationships with Christ. He is much in demand as a conference speaker on evangelism and Christian leadership.

Eims' concern for some years has been the development of leaders committed to excellence—in their personal lives and as examples to those whom they lead. A combat marine in World War II, Eims has seen firsthand the results of excellent and poor leadership—in terms of human lives. In the arena of Christian warfare the best in leadership is demanded.

This book is an outgrowth of Eims' personal study of the Scriptures and his sharing of leadership principles with others. It is chock-full of biblical examples and personal experiences, an outgrowth of his ministry around the world.

He and his wife, Virginia, have three children, Larry, Becky, and Randy.

CONTENTS

Foreword

For nearly two decades I have had the opportunity of observing LeRoy Eims in the role of a leader. I have seen him take young men who seem to be purposeless in life and patiently work with them to produce leaders. I've also seen his leadership in directing training centers to prepare college students for effective Christian service and leadership. Being strong in self-discipline, he has instilled in many of them a truly disciplined life.

Mr. Eims is a good Bible student and has based the contents of this book on sound biblical principles. By precept, he first shows God's methods of leadership. Then he illustrates these precepts by biblical examples as well as by many personal experiences. In other words, he's not teaching idealism but principles of leadership based on the Bible and experience in personal life.

It will be well for Christian workers and leaders to read and reread this book and to put into practice these proven, basic principles of spiritual leadership. I also believe this book can serve well as a guide for leaders to use in training others.

I thus highly recommend this book to believers everywhere.

Theodore H. Epp
Founder
Back to the Bible Broadcast

Preface

In 1956 my wife and I were asked by Dawson Trotman, the founder and director of The Navigators, to go to Omaha, Nebraska, and open up The Navigator Ministry in the Midwest.

My prime responsibility was to win men and women to Christ, disciple those who responded to the Gospel, and train those disciples to repeat the process in the lives of others. Second Timothy 2:2 became a guide: "And the things you have heard me say in the presence of many witnesses, entrust to reliable men who will also be qualified to teach others."

In addition to this basic ministry, I was to recruit and send leaders to fill the ranks of men and women who would take the message of the Gospel to the uttermost part of the earth.

I determined to do a study on leadership to help me train twelve potential leaders who were part of our ministry.

To begin this study on leadership, I checked out twenty-five books from the Omaha Public Library and spent the day going over them. From these twenty-five books I chose twelve and gave them to the twelve men I was training in leadership. After one month we all gathered for a day of sharing what we had learned from the books we had read.

About halfway through the day, a startling truth began to unveil itself. As I listened to these young, potential leaders recount what they had learned from these books, it dawned on me that most of the major points on leadership these books contained were in the Bible.

That began a nineteen-year study of the Scriptures on the subject of leadership and resulted in this book.

I trust these lessons on leadership will be of help to you in your walk with God and your service for Him.

LeRoy Eims

Chapter One

Who Is
Fit to Lead?

Before people take on a leadership responsibility, they should weigh the matter carefully. "Not many of you should presume to be teachers, my brothers, because you know that we who teach will be judged more strictly" (James 3:1). Leaders will be held in more severe and stricter judgment than their followers. That one thought should give us pause.

The next sentence in that same chapter gives another reason: "For in many things we offend all" (KJV). We know that we make many a slip; we stumble in so many ways. That being the case, we are naturally hesitant to presume to lead others.

However, it is evident in analyzing the lives of God's leaders that this feeling of inadequacy is not a good reason for declining the job. After all, we are all sinners before God. Who among us could claim that we have not blown it in many ways and in many different situations? If that is an adequate reason for not stepping up and taking the lead, no one would ever do so.

Let's look at some of God's chosen leaders of the past and see how they responded when the Lord approached them to take the lead in a task.

The Call of Moses

Take a look at Moses. He was in the backside of the desert keeping the flock of Jethro, his father-in-law, when God's call came. The very fact that this highly educated man, who had been accustomed to the comforts and pleasures of the palace, was occupied in one of the lowliest pursuits of his day could have been enough to embitter him. Herding sheep was a profession held in low esteem. He could have been moping around feeling sorry for himself, so occupied with his misery and ill fortune as to miss the voice of God completely. To top it off, he was working for his in-laws!

Then a strange and wonderful thing happened. "There the angel of the Lord appeared to him in flames of fire from within a bush. Moses saw that though the bush was on fire it did not burn up" (Ex. 3:2).

The first thing the Lord did was reveal Himself to Moses. Moses was certain that it was God who spoke to him (see vv. 5-6). This is something that you must be sure about in your own mind. When someone comes to ask you to serve in one way or another, make certain that God is in it. Don't budge an inch in either direction — either yes or no — until you have determined the will of God in the matter.

Sometimes you will know God's will immediately. Other times you will have to wait until God makes it plain to you. But be assured of this — God will show you. Our Father in heaven is well able to communicate to His children. God will confirm His will in the matter to you. He does not want us to spend our lives in uncertainty.

Since God is concerned with what we do, He will make His will known. He promises to do so. "I will instruct you and teach you in the way you should go; I will counsel you and watch over you" (Ps. 32:8). In this verse, notice the pronoun *I*, referring to God, appears twice. Guidance is God's responsibility. The assurance of guidance is as basic in Scripture as is the assurance of forgiveness. Notice also God says, "I *will* instruct. I *will* teach. I *will* guide." He will show us the way to go. Blessed assurance!

Another promise is found in Psalm 48:14: "For this God is our God for ever and ever; He will be our guide even to the end." The words of this promise are unmistakable: "He will be our guide." So you can rely on His willingness and ability to show you what His will is for you. Like Moses, you can be certain that God has spoken.

The next thing that occurred was that the Lord revealed to Moses the burden that He had for His people. "The Lord said, 'I have indeed seen the misery of My people in Egypt. I have heard them crying out because of their slave drivers, and I am concerned about their suffering' " (Ex. 3:7). Moses, you recall, had been burdened over the plight of the Children of Israel, and it was an encouragement for him to realize that God Himself was concerned for them as well.

Then God made a dramatic statement: "So I have come down to rescue them from the hand of the Egyptians and to bring them up out of that land into a good and spacious land, a land flowing with milk and honey" (v. 8). Can you imagine the joy and excitement that must have flooded Moses' mind at that point? The living God was going to personally take a hand and deliver the people!

Then the Lord made a statement that must have thrown Moses into confusion. "So now, go. I am sending you to Pharaoh to bring My people the Israelites out of Egypt" (v. 10). Can't you just hear the questions flooding Moses' mind? "But Lord, I thought You said *You* were going to come down and deliver them. Why then this idea that I should go to Pharaoh and that *I* should bring forth the Children of Israel out of Egypt? If You are going to do it, Lord, why do *I* need to go?"

That, by the way, is a key question all of us must get answered in our own mind. When we understand that God's *method* of accomplishing His plan and purposes is *people,* we will begin to understand our role in the kingdom of God.

So it was with Moses. God had a job for him. However, Moses did not feel qualified for the task that God had given him. And he cried out to God with his question, "Who am I?"

Now frankly, that is not all that hard of a question for God. He could have simply answered, "You are Moses." But the question was so irrelevant that God did not even bother to answer it.

Therein lies one of the great secrets of leadership in the Christian enterprise. God said, "Certainly I will be with you."

What the Lord was trying to get across to Moses was a powerful truth. He as much as said, "Moses, it doesn't really matter
who you are — whether you feel qualified or unqualified, whether you feel up to the task or not. The point is that *I* am going
to be there. The statement I made to you still holds: 'I have
come down to rescue them.' I am going to do it, and I am going
to give you the privilege of being in it with Me. You will be My
instrument of deliverance."

By all means, remember this truth when God calls you to
take a position of leadership in His work. God is not looking
for people who feel "sufficient." Paul said, "Not that we are
competent to claim anything for ourselves, but our competence comes from God" (2 Cor. 3:5).

I'm sure the sense of need and inadequacy can be an asset
rather than a handicap. Paul's testimony bears this out: "But
He said to me, 'My grace is sufficient for you, for My power is
made perfect in weakness.' Therefore I will boast all the more
gladly about my weaknesses, so that Christ's power may rest
on me. . . . For when I am weak, then I am strong" (12:9-10).

Many people are amazed at that and say, "Do you mean the
great Apostle Paul felt that way?" The answer is yes, and that
no doubt contributed to his greatness.

The next lesson we learn in our look at the call of Moses is
an important one as well. It is right to be aware of our inadequacy, but we mustn't stop there. We must also be convinced
of the absolute sufficiency of God. That's God's next step in
dealing with Moses.

Moses came up with another question: "Suppose I go to the
Israelites and say to them, 'The God of your fathers has sent
me to you,' and they ask me, 'What is His name?' Then what
shall I tell them?" (Ex. 3:13)

To this God gives a remarkable answer: "I am who I am.
This is what you are to say to the Israelites: 'I AM has sent me
to you. . . . The Lord, The God of your fathers — the God of
Abraham, the God of Isaac and the God of Jacob — has sent me
to you.' This is My name forever, the name by which I am to
be remembered from generation to generation" (vv. 14-15).

As a young Christian I puzzled over that answer for a long

time. What did God mean when He revealed Himself as "I AM"? Then one day it hit me. God is saying, "Whatever you need, that's what I am!"

At this point in his life, Moses needed encouragement and strength. Quite possibly that will be your need when you receive your call from God to serve Him in some specific task.

More important, the fact that we are never without needs brings this truth into focus. Do we need comfort? *I am* your comfort: "Cast all your anxiety on Him because He cares for you" (1 Peter 5:7). Do we need victory over some sin that plagues us? *I am* your victory. "But thanks be to God! He gives us the victory through our Lord Jesus Christ" (1 Cor. 15:57). Do we need love? "God is love" (1 John 4:8). And so on down the catalog of needs. God is absolutely sufficient to meet them. What God was saying was *I am all that My people need.*

So it's true that we must acknowledge our insufficiency, but it must not stop there. If it does, we are in trouble. We must go on to acknowledge the absolute adequacy and sufficiency of God to meet any test, to overcome any problem, and to win any victory. It took Moses a little time, but he did come to that point and was mightily used of God.

The Call of Gideon

To reinforce in our minds this absolutely essential truth of God's sufficiency, let's consider another man at the point of his call from God. Remember the great battles that were waged and won by Gideon? With a handful of men he "turned to flight the armies of the aliens." Was he always like that? Bold, courageous, waxing valiant in a fight?

Hardly!

The Children of Israel were suffering under the hand of the Midianites. They were hiding in dens and caves in the mountains. The Midianites destroyed their crops and confiscated their livestock. These enemies, like a plague of grasshoppers, consumed everything as they moved across the land. The reason for Israel's dilemma was, of course, their sin. "Again the Israelites did evil in the eyes of the Lord, and for seven years

He gave them into the hands of the Midianites" (Jud. 6:1).

One night Gideon was threshing a little wheat to hide it from the Midianites. The angel of the Lord appeared and called upon him to be the instrument to deliver God's people out of the hand of the Midianites.

Gideon's first response was quite familiar to God by this time. "But Lord . . . how can I save Israel? My clan is the weakest in Manasseh, and I am the least in my family" (v. 15).

Again, God went to the heart of the matter with His chosen man for the job. "I will be with you, and you will strike down all the Midianites together" (v. 16).

Notice the similarity to what God told Moses at the burning bush. In effect, God said, "Gideon, it doesn't matter that your family is poor in Manasseh, or that you are least in your father's house. The point is not who you are, but that *I* will be with you. It is not your weakness that we must dwell on, but My strength. I will work through you."

So, if God calls you to a task and you have an overpowering sense of weakness and need and inadequacy—rejoice! You're in good company. People of God down through the centuries have felt the same way. But they have also believed God to be sufficient for the task to which He has called them.

The Call of Jeremiah

There is one more person we must look at to round out this matter. Jeremiah was one of the great prophets of God. He was faithful to God's call and suffered for that faithfulness. But how did the call come? And how did Jeremiah respond when God spoke to him about assuming a position of leadership in His kingdom? Look at the record: "The word of the Lord came to me, saying, 'Before I formed you in the womb I knew you, before you were born I set you apart; I appointed you as a prophet to the nations' " (Jer. 1:4-5).

The basic job of a prophet was to proclaim the Word of God to the people of God. How did Jeremiah respond to this challenge? Did he immediately rise to the occasion with faith and enthusiasm? No, his response was similar to those of Moses and Gideon: " 'Ah, Sovereign Lord,' I said, 'I do not know how to speak; I am only a child' " (v. 6). His initial reaction was one of inadequacy. He didn't feel equal to the task.

Here's God's answer to that: "But the Lord said to me, 'Do not say, "I am only a child." You must go to everyone I send you to and say whatever I command you. Do not be afraid of them, for I am with you and will rescue you,' declares the Lord" (vv. 7-8). Notice the promise of God: "I am with you." Again, the point is that God is there. The all-wise, all-powerful, all-sufficient God will be by his side. In every case, this is the thing God keeps saying.

In the case of Jeremiah, God did not promise him a rose garden, but the assurance of His presence and protection and guidance was given time and again: " 'They will fight against you but will not overcome you, for I am with you and will rescue you,' declares the Lord" (v. 19).

Other Calls – Then and Now

Do you recall the last orders of the Lord Jesus Christ to His followers? "Go and make disciples of all nations." Accompanying that charge to them was the promise, "I am with you always" (Matt. 28:19-20). God is still giving us the same basis for serving Him with confidence that He gave to old-time heroes of the faith: *I am with you.*

Some years ago I was asked to speak at a Sunday School class retreat. For years Jim Rayburn, founder of the Young Life movement, had been teacher of the Mr. and Mrs. Class at First Presbyterian Church of Colorado Springs. The class was having its annual retreat, and they called on The Navigators for a speaker. Rod Sargent, to whom the request had first come, was unable to go, so he called me into his office and suggested I do it.

I froze. For a class taught by Jim Rayburn? What had I to offer to a class that had this man of God for a regular teacher? "Behold I cannot speak, I thought to myself, "for I am a child." I was only about six or seven years old in the Lord at the time, and most of the people there would be my elders both physically and spiritually. So I began to explain all this to Rod and asked him to get someone else.

Rod sat there looking at me and didn't say anything for quite a while. Then he spoke. "LeRoy," he said, "one thing I've noticed about you. You always seem to want to take the course of least resistance. You shy away from something that may be difficult or require a real step of faith." Then he told me to think about it for a while and pray about it.

I did. Though I *still* felt inadequate for the task, the Lord definitely spoke to me about accepting it. Needless to say, I prepared with much study and hours of prayer.

To my delight the retreat went quite well. I sensed the presence and guidance of God and His enabling power. The Lord taught me some very helpful lessons through that situation — not the least of which was the truth of God's admonition that I must not move through life taking the course of least resistance. The experience was good for me, hard but valuable down through the years.

Another thing the devil may use to prevent us from stepping out by faith in response to the call of God is something undesirable in our background. We may feel this disadvantage is too much to overcome or that it will be a hindrance to the work. Again, the Scriptures remind us of the fallacy of this argument.

The Apostle Paul, you recall, was a murderer who had spent a great deal of time and energy persecuting the church of God. He later confessed with shame: "These men know that I went from one synagogue to another to imprison and beat those who believe in You. And when the blood of Your martyr Stephen was shed, I stood there giving my approval and guarding the clothes of those who were killing him" (Acts 22:19-20).

Paul said of himself, "I am the least of the apostles and do not even deserve to be called an apostle, because I persecuted the church of God" (1 Cor. 15:9). But he also wrote, "I thank Christ Jesus our Lord, who has given me strength, that He considered me faithful, appointing me to His service. Even though I was once a blasphemer and a persecutor and a violent man, I was shown mercy because I acted in ignorance and unbelief" (1 Tim. 1:12-13).

If ever a man had a background that would render him unusable to God, it was Paul. Yet he became the great apostle to the Gentiles and was used of God to write much of the New Testament.

Other people with dark blots on their records became great servants of God as well. I think of John Mark, the man who proved to be an unfaithful servant on a journey with Paul and Barnabas. When these men planned their next journey, Paul refused to take Mark along because of his past failure (see Acts 15:36-38).

Yet this is the man whom God chose to write the Gospel of Mark, which presents His own Son as the ever faithful servant. Mark's background was certainly not the thing that was the basis for God's choosing him for the task.

David was chosen by God to be the commander and leader of His people and to be administrative head of the government. His background was that of a shepherd tending the sheep on the rolling hills of the land of Israel. But God called him and he followed. His background, or lack of it, was not an issue.

So when God calls you to a task, let neither a sense of inadequacy or a "poor background" hinder you from following His lead. "For it is God who works in you to will and to act according to His good purpose" (Phil. 2:13).

Chapter Two

The Leader's Source of Power

A power failure can be disastrous. Hospitals and other vital facilities have their backup systems of generators in case the power fails. This equipment must keep functioning because lives depend on it. Power and the means to use it are critical to an industrialized society.

Leaders must be aware of this. They must realize that they must keep their program, their people, and themselves moving. What is the leader's source of power for all this? God Himself.

Fellowship

The Apostle Paul said to one of his supporting churches, "I can do everything through Him who gives me strength" (Phil. 4:13). David centuries earlier said, "It is God who arms me with strength and makes my way perfect" (2 Sam. 22:33). God Himself is our source of power, but *fellowship* with God is that which "throws the switch," and makes that power operative and effective in our lives. The greatest preparation for David's leadership as king was his time spent alone with God as a shepherd boy in the Judean hills.

Years alone *with* God prepared David for leadership *under* God. He certainly saw leadership in operation firsthand while living in the palace as a youth, but his time with God was of greater value to him than his time with people. As the leader of his army and administrator of the nation, he had little preparation. He had no courses in ROTC. He did not take Business Administration 101, but he knew God.

This area, also, is where the devil strikes the hardest. He may take mild interest in your attendance at leadership seminars or in your subscription to *Business Week*. But when you get serious about knowing God through vital fellowship with Him, he mounts an all-out attack to prevent it. You will find your schedule disrupted and many urgent matters to consider. You will be much too busy to fellowship with the Lord.

Why does the enemy of our souls fight time with God so furiously? Because of its imperative nature in the life of the leader. What are the spiritual rewards that come our way, we might ask, if we are faithful to our fellowship with God? To answer that question we must ask another. What is man's ultimate purpose on earth? The answer: ". . . everyone who is called by My name, whom I created for My glory, whom I formed and made." "Man's chief end is to glorify God and to enjoy Him forever." Often people recite that statement of the Westminster Shorter Catechism, but they really don't know what it means in daily life.

I recall discussing that with a group of seminary students. They knew that our purpose for being on earth was to glorify God. I asked one of them what a person did to accomplish that. How *do* you glorify God? His face took on a quizzical look and, with a grin that was prompted more by shame than humor, he said, "I haven't the faintest idea." Imagine that! Here was a group of students preparing for spiritual leadership, and they had no idea of how to accomplish their primary goal in life.

Let me share with you a simple lesson I learned as a young Christian. God originally created people to glorify His name. He created humans in His own image for fellowship with Himself. God had a close relationship with Adam and Eve in the garden. But then they sinned. They disobeyed God. They brought dishonor to His name. The image was marred and the fellowship broken. When the time was just right, however, God took a decisive step to re-create people's potential to bring glory to His name.

Was there ever a person whose every thought, word, and deed brought glory to God every hour of every day of every year of his or her life? Yes. One. The Lord Jesus Christ. In Jesus' prayer to His Father, He said of Himself, "I have brought You glory on earth by completing the work You gave Me to do" (John 17:4). Therefore, if I am ever to accomplish my ultimate goal in life, to glorify God, I must be transformed more and more into His image, to become like Christ.

The desire of God's heart is for us to become like His Son. "For those God foreknew He also predestined to be conformed to the likeness of His Son, that He might be the firstborn among many brothers" (Rom. 8:29). This glorifies God.

How then do I become like Christ? How does a person become like another? By being around the person, talking with that person, doing things together. Have you ever seen a picture of a couple who have lived together for fifty years and are celebrating their golden wedding anniversary? They not only act alike and enjoy the same things and have the same tastes; they even look alike!

I remember the day when Lt. Al Vail of the U.S. Marine Corps married Margie Igo, a charming, beautiful, intelligent graduate of Stanford. They had met at a Christian conference in Colorado, and Al fell head over heels in love with Margie. In typical Marine fashion he launched a campaign to win her. Letters, phone calls, flowers, and gifts began to arrive.

At first Margie was a bit startled by it all, but after some months the Lord confirmed in her heart that Al was God's choice for her. So they were married. A little over a year after the wedding I visited them in their home in Virginia.

When I arrived, Margie apologized because I had to wait a few minutes for her to prepare my room. In her words, the room was not "squared away" yet.

"Squared away!" I thought. Stanford grads don't go about squaring things away. But this Stanford grad did because she had lived for a year with Lt. Al Vail, USMC, who made it his business to see that everything and everyone around him was "squared away." She had begun to pick up his mannerisms. Then Al came home, and I was startled to see how Margie's life had also affected him. They had lived together in fellowship with each other and were becoming like each other.

So it is with us in our relationship with the Lord. For us to be "conformed to the image of Jesus Christ," we must invest much time alone with Him in personal fellowship. Leaders who will do this, who have a "built-in" devotional life rather than one that is "tacked on," will find themselves in vital touch with God and be mightily used of God. God searches for such people. "I looked for a man among them who would build up the wall and stand before Me in the gap on behalf of the land so I would not have to destroy it, but I found none" (Ezek. 22:30). This hunt is as new as our unborn sons and daughters and as old as the dawn of humanity. When God finds a person who will place as his or her first priority a life of intimate, personal, dynamic fellowship with Him, He directs His power, guidance, and wisdom into and through that person. God has found a person through whom He can change the world.

The Word of God

Three basic elements characterize a life of fellowship with the Lord. God speaks to us by means of His Word. "All Scripture is God-breathed and is useful for teaching, rebuking, correcting, and training in righteousness, so that the man of God may be thoroughly equipped for every good work" (2 Tim. 3:16-17).

We must get into the Word and the Word must get into us. We get into the Word by hearing it preached, reading it, studying it, and memorizing it. We get the Word into us through meditation. By meditating on it, we assimilate the Word of God into our spiritual lives. Like physical food, it is not what we take in that affects us but what we digest and assimilate. That's meditation. To meditate is to go deeply into the Word, to revolve it in our minds, to go below the surface. "Oh, how I love Your law! I meditate on it all day long" (Ps. 119:97).

In 1963 I visited London on a preaching tour. The schedule allowed us a day of sightseeing. David Limebear, a young man on our university team there, was assigned to be our tour guide and was eager to show us the sights and sounds of his beloved city. David arrived early in the morning armed with a list of historic places and the subway schedule. He had it all figured out, exactly when the underground railway would arrive at each point, how much time we had there, and when we had to leave to catch the next train for the next stop.

I entered into this sightseeing with the sort of excitement you'd expect to find in a boy from Neola, Iowa, about to see the big city. David was the athletic type in top physical shape, and he kept us on the move. We jogged through the cathedrals, sprinted through the parks, paused momentarily to gaze at the statues, and cast hasty glances at buildings that oozed grandeur and history. We really saw London—but did we?

Some years later my wife and I were there on another preaching assignment, and our last day was spent with some people seeing the sights. The pace was leisurely. I saw and absorbed the beauty and majesty of the cathedrals I had jogged through some years before. This time my spirits were affected. I had time to really see them, to experience them, to sense the meaning and the message in them.

So it is with the Word of God. If we hurry through an assigned Bible reading, if we quickly grind out a Bible study for our group in a Sunday School class, if we're looking at our watch hoping the service will end so we can run to something else, little will happen in our lives. It's like jogging through a cathedral. We see it, but we don't really. But if we open the Word and take time to let the Spirit of God affect our lives, to absorb it into our souls, to see its beauty and grandeur, we will be in true fellowship with God.

God wants to communicate with us through His Word. If we take time to meditate, we will experience the depth and the greatness of the message, and the Spirit of God will speak to us and affect our lives. And here's an important point. It is God who does it, not the words printed on paper. God uses His Word as a means, as an instrument to communicate Himself to us. "I am laid low in the dust; renew my life according to Your Word" (Ps. 119:25). Note that it was God Himself who could breathe new life into the psalmist. He used His Word as an instrument to do it.

We need to develop a love for the word of God. "Oh, how I love Your law! I meditate on it all day long" (Ps. 119:97). It was love for the Word of God that prompted the psalmist's meditation on the Word. That's the place to start. Ask God to give you a love for and delight in His Word. "Direct me in the path of Your commands, for there I find delight" (v. 35). "Praise the Lord. Blessed is the man who fears the Lord, who finds great delight in His commands" (112:1). "I delight in Your commandments because I love them" (119:47).

Leaders who are worth their salt and who will truly lead others spiritually must be a person of the Word.

Prayer

The second element of fellowship is prayer. God speaks to us through His Word and we speak to Him through prayer. The thing to remember is that there are prayers that move the hand of God and there are prayers that have no effect at all. What's the difference?

Jesus talked about the different kinds of praying in a parable.

> Two men went up to the temple to pray, one a Phari-see and the other a tax collector. The Pharisee stood up and prayed about himself: "God, I thank You that I am not like other men — robbers, evildoers, adulter-ers — or even like this tax collector. I fast twice a week and give a tenth of all I get." But the tax collector stood at a distance. He would not even look up to heaven, but beat his breast and said, "God, have mercy on me, a sinner." I tell you that this man, rather than the other, went home justified before God. For every-one who exalts himself will be humbled, and he who humbles himself will be exalted (Luke 18:10-14).

One summer I had the privilege of hearing a concert on the Potomac River in Washington, D.C. The orchestra was per-forming the *1812 Overture.* At one point in it there is cannon fire. The cannons don't try to hit anything; they just "fire for effect." It adds drama and excitement to the overture.

I recall my days in the Marine Corps during World War II as a forward observer in an artillery unit. One of the pieces would fire a round, and I would observe where it landed in relationship to the target. I would then radio a message to raise or lower, go right or left. They would fire another round, and I would give new instructions. Finally, I would give the final instruction and call on them to "fire for effect."

I used the same expression as that relating to the overture, but meant something far different. At that point the entire battery would open up on the target with devastating effect.

So it is in the parable of Jesus. The Pharisee was merely praying for effect, as a means to impress, and Jesus said, "He prayed thus with himself." The publican, on the other hand, did business with God. He prayed for effect, to accomplish something. This is the kind of prayer we should offer to God. "The prayer of a righteous man is powerful and effective" (James 5:16). For a prayer to be effectual, it must be fervent.

This is illustrated by an incident in the Early Church (Acts 12:1-12). King Herod had begun a reign of terror and persecution against Christians. He had killed James, the brother of John, and was about to kill Peter also. Peter was in prison securely guarded by sixteen soldiers. But prayer was made for him by the Christians; and in response to that prayer, the Lord sent an angel to release him.

Various translations use different words to describe the kind of prayer that was offered. The word that is used to describe the prayer is the word that is used to describe the intensity of feeling one has when being pulled apart on a torture rack.

The reason for this fervent prayer is obvious. First, it was physically impossible for Peter to escape. The main thing that prompted their fervent prayer, however, was Peter's past. He was known to have denied the Lord when the going got rough. Was God answering their prayers? Abundantly! The night before his execution Peter was sleeping like a baby, chained between two soldiers. The effectual fervent prayer of this little band of Christians availed much. Not only had Peter not defected, but also he was released from prison in a most remarkable way. God heard and answered.

I made a house call with a doctor a few years ago. When the doctor completed his examination, he said, "The man has a bad heart." I asked myself, how did he know? The man could have said that he never felt better, the old ticker was in good shape, and the doctor was wasting his time talking to him about it. But no matter what the man might have said, Dr. Frank knew he had a bad heart. How? Simple. He listened to the man's heart with a stethoscope and paid no attention to what the man was saying.

So it is with God. We don't pray into a spiritual microphone with God listening on a set of heavenly earphones. He listens to us pray with a spiritual stethoscope. "These people honor Me with their lips, but their hearts are far from Me" (Matt. 15:8). Jeremiah's call to "pour out your heart like water in the presence of the Lord" (Lam. 2:19) must be heeded today.

Have you ever heard Christians say when they part, "I'll be praying for you." How often it is merely a way of saying good-bye. How different were the words of the Apostle Paul, "God, whom I serve with my whole heart in preaching the Gospel of His Son, is my witness how constantly I remember you in my prayers at all times" (Rom. 1:9-10).

For prayer to be fervent it must be specific. Too often we fall into the rut of praying, "God bless the church," or "God encourage the missionaries," or "God help the class." The leaders' praying must be specific in two areas.

First, the leaders' prayers should concentrate on the growth and development of each of the people whom they lead. The Apostle Paul gave us an example:

> For this reason, since the day we heard about you, we have not stopped praying for you and asking God to fill you with the knowledge of His will through all spiritual wisdom and understanding. And we pray this in order that you may live a life worthy of the Lord and may please Him in every way: bearing fruit in every good work, growing in the knowledge of God (Col. 1:9-10).

Likewise, consider the prayers of Epaphras. "Epaphras, who is one of you and a servant of Christ Jesus, sends greetings.

He is always wrestling in prayer for you, that you may stand firm in all the will of God, mature and fully assured" (4:12). Second, leaders should pray for the spiritual maturity of their people and that God might raise up from their midst laborers to go into the harvest fields of the world.

> When He saw the crowds, He had compassion on them, because they were harassed and helpless, like sheep without a shepherd. Then He said to His disciples, "The harvest is plentiful but the workers are few. Ask the Lord of the harvest, therefore, to send out workers into His harvest field" (Matt. 9:36-38).

Obedience

The last element of fellowship is obedience. There is no fellowship with a superior apart from obedience to him or her, and Jesus Christ is very much our Superior.

Before I became a Christian, I spent some time on the island of Pavuvu with the First Marine Division during World War II. Pavuvu was our rest camp between invasions. And what a rest camp it was! The island was infested with blow flies, red ants, rats, and mosquitoes. Our tents leaked, and in the mornings we would often find land crabs in our boots. The heat was oppressive, and the daily rain was a nuisance. We had nothing but "C" rations to eat.

To make life a bit more bearable, the Marine Corps provided one can of beer a month, much to the delight of us beer drinkers. Though we welcomed this monthly treat, it hardly filled the bill for those of us who were used to beer as a steady diet. So I hit upon a little scheme. When the beer ration was given, I worked it out with the nondrinkers to sell me theirs. This was strictly against regulations, of course, but in our outfit it was well recognized that a good conduct medal meant four years of undetected rule breaking.

I would take my twelve to fifteen cans of warm beer back to my tent, sit in the middle of the floor, poke them open with a rusty Japanese bayonet, and start consuming the contents. After eight to ten cans, I would usually get a bit unsteady and would begin shaking the can a bit before opening it. One day I dropped a can a couple of times, finally got it upright, and hit it with the bayonet. It spurted a stream of warm beer — all over my commanding officer who at that moment had stepped into my tent. There he stood, drenched from head to foot with my warm beer. Somehow, for the next few weeks, he and I didn't experience the warmth of fellowship that we had known.

There *is* no fellowship with a superior apart from obedience. Jesus said, "Whoever has My commands and obeys them, he is the one who loves Me. He who loves Me will be loved by My Father, and I too will love him and show Myself to him" (John 14:21).

The Lord clearly spelled out the danger of disobedience.

> Why do you call Me, "Lord, Lord," and do not do what I say? I will show you what he is like who comes to Me and hears My words and puts them into practice. He is like a man building a house, who dug down deep and laid the foundation on rock. When a flood came, the torrent struck that house but could not shake it, because it was well built. But the one who hears My words and does not put them into practice is like a man who built a house on the ground without a foundation. The moment the torrent struck that house, it collapsed and its destruction was complete (Luke 6:46-49).

A life of obedience by leaders is the greatest motivation to the people who follow them. They see their lives and are challenged to greater heights of commitment and obedience.

The three elements of fellowship are the Word, prayer, and obedience. They are imperative for leaders. Leaders need to experience the power of God in their lives and ministries on a day-by-day basis. Fellowship with the Lord is the switch that completes the connection and makes that power available. Without it leaders are nothing more than organizers of human effort and activity. With it they are tools in the hands of Almighty God to be used to accomplish His purposes on this earth.

Chapter Three

The Inner Life of the Leader

The Babylonians were a brutal people. Their code of morality and justice was strange and foreign to the captive Hebrews. Killing a human being to them was no different than swatting a fly. Yet here were the Hebrews, terror-stricken slaves in that cruel land, confronted by rules, regulations, and demands that were contrary to everything they had been taught from their youth. They were up against what appeared to be insurmountable odds; yet one of their number would rise to a position of power and authority — in an empire filled with violence, superstition, and the worship of false gods. During the years of his captivity, this man would be called upon by pagan kings to serve in the highest appointive office in the land. The most remarkable thing of all is that he was a man of unbending principle who worshiped the living and true God. We can learn much by looking at the inner life of this remarkable leader.

Daniel was only a youth when he was chosen by King Nebuchadnezzar for a special assignment. He was one of a small group to whom the king was to teach "the language and literature of the Babylonians" (Dan. 1:4). He and his three companions were part of an elite band with very special qualifications: "Young men without any physical defect, handsome, showing aptitude for every kind of learning, well-informed, quick to understand, and qualified to serve in the king's palace" (v. 4). Stated in contemporary language, they were physically fit, socially desirable, practically intelligent (they had horse sense), intellectually sharp, educationally equipped, and diplomatically capable.

Any dean of admissions of any college or university would look at this list of qualifications and welcome such youths to the student body. Corporations would drool at the prospect of getting young men like these in their employ. But here's an interesting thing: God raised up only one of them to the place of greatest spiritual leadership. Why? Because of certain basic qualities in the inner life of this man. Let us examine three of the most important.

Purity of Life

A primary characteristic exhibited by Daniel was purity of life. "But Daniel resolved not to defile himself" (Dan. 1:8). It is interesting to note that one of the first things God did at the dawn of creation was to divide the light from the darkness. That act symbolizes a great spiritual truth: you're either on one side or the other — there's no room for fence-straddling.

In hell there is no light, and in heaven there is no darkness. We, who have given our lives to Christ, having experienced His love and forgiveness, will one day live with Him in heaven; we will enter His mansions and bask in His presence. In preparation for that great day, we ought to get used to walking in the light while on this earth.

The Apostle Paul continues this theme: "Do not be yoked together with unbelievers. For what do righteousness and wickedness have in common? Or what fellowship can light have with darkness? What harmony is there between Christ and Belial? What does a believer have in common with an unbeliever? What agreement is there between the temple of God and idols? For we are the temple of the living God" (2 Cor. 6:14-16).

Paul used the five questions just quoted to draw a line of demarcation between God and the opposition. On one side he gathers righteousness, light, Christ, faith, and the house of God. On the other he lists lawlessness, darkness, Satan, unbelief, and false worship. He states that you cannot mix these two lists. You must choose to live on one side or the other. This is an obvious truth; yet many of us attempt to compromise with sin. Leaders must set an example in their own behavior that matches the standard of Scripture: "The overseer must be above reproach" (1 Tim. 3:2).

The Lord takes note of the inner life of the leader, and it has always been so. When God had rejected King Saul and was choosing his successor, He said to Samuel, "Do not consider his appearance or his height, for I have rejected him. The Lord does not look at the things man looks at. Man looks at the outward appearance, but the Lord looks at the heart" (1 Sam. 16:7). You and I tend to evaluate people by superficial standards: only what we see. God looks inside.

A few years ago a violent windstorm hit our city. It blew out plate-glass windows in the downtown stores and banks. Herb Lockyer, the man who taught our Sunday School class for many years, and his wife Ardis were driving home when she saw something that caused her heart to sink. One of the most beautiful trees in town had been uprooted by the wind. She called it to Herb's attention and then exclaimed, "Look Herb! That tree is rotten on the inside."

It was true. This tree that had been admired for its grandeur and beauty was completely eaten out on the inside. And because it was rotten within, there came a day when it faced a wind it could not withstand. It toppled, and people who had appreciated its huge branches and beautiful leaves learned the truth. In spite of the fact that outwardly it was a thing of beauty, inwardly it was rotten.

So it is with our lives. If the Christian leader tries to put on an outward show with no inward fortification of purity and holiness before God, one day a test will reveal his or her true nature and character. Thus, the leader *must* live a pure life.

Paul shares with Timothy another reason for moral purity.

> Everyone who confesses the name of the Lord must turn away from wickedness. In a large house there are articles not only of gold and silver, but also of wood and

clay; some are for noble purposes and some for igno-
ble. If a man cleanses himself from the latter, he will
be an instrument for noble purposes, made holy, useful
to the Master and prepared to do any good work
(2 Tim. 2:19-21).

This passage points out a truth that is obvious in our homes.
Various receptacles have various uses. In my home we have
one container for garbage and another that is used as a salad
bowl. And my wife doesn't mix them up and change them
around. The simple spiritual truth is that people can choose
which kind of vessel they will be in the household of God. It is
up to them to be vessels unto honor or dishonor. The criteria
by which God decides whom He will use for which of His
eternal purposes on earth are spelled out at the end (v. 21):
those who purge themselves of dishonorable characteristics
will be vessels unto honor.

Some years ago my wife's uncle Art gave her a lovely set of
old crystal glasses. These occupy a place of honor in our
household and are used only on very special occasions. Suppose you were visiting me and became thirsty. I would take
you to the kitchen and invite you to help yourself to a cool
refreshing drink from the faucet. As you opened the cupboard
to get a glass, you would see that each of these fine crystal
glasses was smeared and dirty. Right in front of you on the
counter you'd see a plain old peanut butter jar that was as
clean as a whistle. Which one would you use?

The answer is obvious. Well, you are no smarter than God.
He is looking for a life that is clean and pure. Then that life
will be "a vessel unto honor, sanctified, and meet for the Master's use, perfected unto every good work."

Notice the word *sanctified*. Much disagreement exists
among God's people regarding that word, but all will agree that
one of its basic meanings is "to be set apart." Let me illustrate. I have a friend who is a ranking officer in the Marine
Corps. Wherever he is stationed, he is given a jeep for his
personal use. This jeep is always available to him, and he
knows where it is when he needs it. Woe be to any young

second lieutenant who would take that jeep for his own purposes. That jeep is *sanctified.* It belongs to the major and is for his use alone.

The leader whose life is set apart for the Lord has a powerful impact on the world around him or her. God has promised to show Himself to others *through* that leader. " 'I will show the holiness of My great name, which has been profaned among the nations, the name you have profaned among them. Then the nations will know that I am the Lord,' declares the Sovereign Lord, 'when I show Myself holy through you before their eyes' " (Ezek. 36:23).

Often leaders are asked by their people for specifics in determining what is right and what is wrong. They want to lead pure lives but are honestly unsure of some issues. The Bible not only deals in specifics, but also in eternal principles. Four of these have been used by the Lord in my own life.

Shortly after I came to know Christ, I realized that certain habits and practices in my life needed to go. I knew they were wrong and did not honor the Lord. Some other things were not so clear. Were they wrong, or weren't they? The Bible was specific about swearing, stealing, and lying, but what about those doubtful things concerning which the Bible gives no clear word?

Shortly after I began to wonder about this, the Lord gave me three verses of Scripture that have been of tremendous help through the years. They contain "how to know right from wrong" principles. I call them the 6–8–10 principles, because they are found in 1 Corinthians 6, 8, and 10.

1. Is it helpful? " 'Everything is permissible for me' — but not everything is beneficial. 'Everything is permissible for me' — but I will not be mastered by anything" (1 Cor. 6:12). On the basis of that verse, I can ask myself: is it helpful? Is whatever I'm about to do helpful to me *physically,* or will it harm me? Does it help me *mentally,* or does it tend to get my mind on things that draw me into sin? This helped me get guidance with regard to motion pictures, TV programs, and certain books and magazines. And does it help me *spiritually?* Does it help me grow, or does it hurt my spiritual development?

2. Does it get me in its power? Does it enslave me? I concluded from that verse (1 Cor. 6:12) that anything that gets me in its grip—that becomes a habit I cannot break—I should leave alone. I have friends today who are slaves to cigarettes, liquor, and drugs. Paul said, "I will not be mastered by anything" (1 Cor. 6:12).

3. Will it cause others to stumble? "When you sin against your brothers in this way and wound their weak consciences, you sin against Christ. Therefore, if what I eat causes my brother to fall into sin, I will never eat meat again, so that I will not cause him to fall" (1 Cor. 8:12-13). Will my doing this cause others to stumble? Maybe I can handle it, but will it affect others who see me doing it? Will it cause them problems? Will my actions lead them into trouble? No man is an island. What I do is seen and sometimes copied by others. I may be the only example of a Christian that somebody has. So I must think of others when I decide on my activities.

4. Is it glorifying to God? "So whether you eat or drink or whatever you do, do it all for the glory of God" (1 Cor. 10:31). Does this contemplated action glorify God? Note the first question in the Westminster Shorter Catechism. "What is the chief end of man?" The answer: "Man's chief end is to glorify God and to enjoy Him forever." You and I are to live our lives to the praise of His glory. So I must ask myself: Can I do this to the glory of God?

These three passages of Scripture have stood the test of time. They contain lasting principles from the all-knowing and ever-loving God.

The question God asks, then, is what's on the inside? Outward performance will reflect the inner life. Leaders must maintain a godly walk before their people and make frequent application of 1 John 1:9: "If we confess our sins, He is faithful and just and will forgive us our sins and purify us from all unrighteousness."

Humility

Another vital characteristic in considering the inner life of the leader is humility. Facing a situation in which most of us would have been content just to stay alive, Daniel rose to a place of power and influence. Under his leadership the kingdom prospered, and he was able to provide guidance and instruction for the king. Through it all, however, he remained a humble servant of God. Often, when he could have exalted himself, he was content to give all the credit to the Lord.

> Daniel replied, "No wise man, enchanter, magician, or diviner can explain to the king the mystery he has asked about, but there is a God in heaven who reveals mysteries. He has shown King Nebuchadnezzar what will happen in days to come. Your dream and the visions that passed through your mind as you lay on your bed are these: As you were lying there, O king, your mind turned to things to come, and the revealer of mysteries showed you what is going to happen. As for me this mystery has been revealed to me, not because I have greater wisdom than other living men, but so that you, O king, may know the interpretation and that you may understand what went through your mind" (Dan. 2:27-30).

A humble spirit is the hallmark of the person God uses. God requires it in His servants. "I am the Lord; that is My name! I will not give My glory to another or My praise to idols" (Isa. 42:8). When His people deviate from the path in this regard and get proud, God has a way of bringing them back to the straight and narrow.

One summer I had the privilege of visiting the foreign mission field. One of the missionaries there told me a fascinating tale.

It seems that when he left for the field, he considered himself God's gift to the world and to the country where he went. His basic attitude was, "Wait till I get there. I'll show 'em! Once I get there I'll be able to straighten everyone out and get the program really producing." So he arrived and began his work.

Needless to say this attitude toward his coworkers did not especially endear him to their hearts. They saw his proud spirit and were turned off. Worst of all, God took note of it and did not prosper his efforts. Nothing went right. All his visionary plans turned to dust. Scripture says,

> Young men, in the same way be submissive to those who are older. All of you clothe yourselves with humility toward one another, because, "God opposes the proud but gives grace to the humble." Humble yourselves, therefore, under God's mighty hand, that He may lift you up in due time (1 Peter 5:5-6).

God *resists,* not blesses, the proud, and the Lord is a formidable Person to have resisting you! Needless to say, the missionary lost.

The story has a happy ending, however. The man saw the error of his ways, repented of his sin, and began to walk humbly with his God. And his life became a blessing. "He has showed you, O man, what is good. And what does the Lord require of you? To act justly and to love mercy and to walk humbly with your God" (Micah 6:8).

Many passages of Scripture deal with this subject. Here are some crucial ones:

Proverbs 6:16-17: "There are . . . things the Lord hates . . . haughty eyes, a lying tongue, hands that shed innocent blood. . . ." Note what heads the list!

Proverbs 8:13: "To fear the Lord is to hate evil; I hate pride and arrogance, evil behavior and perverse speech." Mark well what is at the top.

Why does God oppose pride so vehemently? Is it just some meaningless guideline that the Lord issues? No, of course not. As with everything else in the Scriptures, when the Lord tries to get us to conform to His standards, it is for our own well-being. The way to a full and happy life is to get our eyes off ourselves and live for others. Leaders will prosper only as they walk in that spirit. Pride is one of the prime tools of the devil to get our eyes on ourselves and off others.

When you are looking at yourself, you become insensitive to the needs of other people. You find yourself going through life hurting others, offending them, using them, and abusing them, perhaps even without knowing it. I have observed this in the life of people in positions of leadership, and it has been a tragic thing to watch their spiritual decline.

Philippians 2:3-4: "Do nothing out of selfish ambition or vain conceit, but in humility consider others better than yourselves. Each of you should look not only to your own interests, but also to the interests of others" (Phil. 2:3-4).

A clear example of the corrosive effect of pride may be seen in the life of Uzziah, one of the kings of Judah. "Uzziah was sixteen years old when he became king, and he reigned in Jerusalem fifty-two years. His mother's name was Jecoliah; she was from Jerusalem" (2 Chron. 26:3). At first his basic heart attitude was pure. "He sought God during the days of Zechariah, who instructed him in the fear of God. As long as he sought the Lord, God gave him success" (v. 5). He became famous and successful. "The Ammonites brought tribute to Uzziah, and his fame spread as far as the border of Egypt, because he had become very powerful" (v. 8). He developed mighty armies, and God blessed him.

Then came the beginning of his downfall. "But after Uzziah became powerful, his pride led to his downfall. He was unfaithful to the Lord his God, and entered the temple of the Lord to burn incense on the altar of incense" (v. 16). The problem? He couldn't manage success. He was overcome by pride. And God struck him down with leprosy.

Leaders must be able to define and communicate their objectives and then determine the best path to follow to reach those goals. Pride is their greatest enemy at that juncture. When people are full of pride, they cannot see the best way of achieving their purposes, for they only see the way that brings *them* the most honor and acclaim. Somehow pride blinds people to finding the best path. Their minds refuse to be that discerning. They see only what their pride wants them to see. And it has deadly consequences.

King Nebuchadnezzar fell because of it. "But when his heart became arrogant and hardened with pride, he was deposed from his royal throne and stripped of his glory" (Dan. 5:20).

On the other hand, Isaiah portrays the kind of person God uses.

> This is what the Lord says: "Heaven is My throne and the earth is My footstool. Where is the house you will build for Me? Where will My resting place be? Has not My hand made all these things, and so they came into being?" declares the Lord. "This is the one I esteem: he who is humble and contrite in spirit, and trembles at My word" (Isa. 66:1-2).

I have heard Billy Graham say on numerous occasions that he gives all the glory to God for whatever is accomplished through his ministry. He states emphatically that if he touches that glory, he is finished.

A proud spirit, therefore, is deadly to leaders. It will kill their effectiveness for God for it breeds two dreadful diseases of the soul. The first is *ignorance*. Pride makes a person self-sufficient and unteachable. It blinds them to their own needs. It causes them to ignore the good advice and counsel of others.

Throughout the Scriptures God directs our attention to the tremendous value of counsel. "Plans fail for lack of counsel, but with many advisers they succeed" (Prov. 15:22).

Spiritual counsel, however, must be that which has the Lord's interest at heart. That which is best for the kingdom of God. Many seek advice only from those who agree with them; others are disappointed because they can't find unbiased counsel. Counsel, even when given by someone who truly loves you and is interested in that which is best for you, can be dead wrong.

I recall discussing this with G. Christian Weiss, a respected missionary statesman. He told me that he would not have gone to the mission field had he listened to the advice of his friends and relatives. They felt he was throwing his life away. They loved him and had *his* best interest in mind.

Leaders must have these things before them when they are

giving and receiving counsel. They must be teachable but not gullible. They must weigh the counsel they receive in the light of the Bible and the welfare of God's kingdom. Their hearts must remain open and teachable to others. "For lack of guidance a nation falls, but many advisers make victory sure" (Prov. 11:14).

The second disease caused by pride is *insecurity.* Leaders with their eyes on themselves have excessive concern about how they appear in the eyes of others. They are constantly measuring themselves by the yardstick of other people's performances. The Word of God states that this is a foolish and unwise practice. "We do not dare to classify or compare ourselves with some who commend themselves. When they measure themselves by themselves and compare themselves with themselves, they are not wise" (2 Cor. 10:12).

Instead of relaxing in the blessed knowledge that "God has arranged the parts in the body, every one of them, just as He wanted them to be," insecure leaders constantly worry about what others think of them. This makes them less effective in their jobs because their eyes are no longer on the objectives. Their coworkers become a threat to them rather than a help.

Two extremes can result. Either they will try to impress others with ambitious plans and big programs designed to "show them what they can do," or they will retreat into inaction. If they launch a big program, it is likely to be prompted by the energy of the flesh and will ultimately fail. I recall watching a man do this with tragic results. It was like watching a giant factory in full production. The dust was flying, the machines were running, the people were busy, but nothing was coming off the assembly line. The leader's insecurity led him to promote a flurry of activity, but it lacked the blessing of God.

The other extreme, of course, is the fear of failure that brings everything to a standstill. Rather than admit their weaknesses and step out in faith, they do nothing. The Apostle Paul realized his own weakness, but found it to be an asset in his work for Christ when he had the proper attitude: "Three times I pleaded with the Lord to take it away from me. But He said to me, 'My grace is sufficient for you, for My power is made perfect in weakness' " (2 Cor. 12:8-9). A humble spirit in the life of the leader is a powerful force in the hands of Almighty God.

How does a leader maintain a humble spirit before the Lord? Many things are involved, of course, but one stands out. To walk humbly before God, a leader needs to live a life of genuine *praise*. In heaven the beings who surround the throne of God cry, "Holy, holy, holy is the Lord God Almighty" (Rev. 4:8). If leaders live in that spirit of praise, they will be reminded of their own sinfulness and weaknesses. But the reminder will not be from an unhealthy introspection. It will come from a heart that is filled with praises to God for His holiness and power. This in turn can be used of God to thrust them out in faith, confident in the promise, "I can do everything through Him who gives me strength" (Phil. 4:13).

Faith

The third vital characteristic in the inner life of the leader is *faith*. The Bible says, "And without faith it is impossible to please God, because anyone who comes to Him must believe that He exists and that He rewards those who earnestly seek Him" (Heb. 11:6). So often we hear that God looks for a childlike faith in His followers. But what is that? What is involved? We will discuss four aspects.

First, faith means that we *believe God will provide*. "And my God will meet all your needs according to His glorious riches in Christ Jesus" (Phil. 4:19). My first assignment as a Christian worker was in Pittsburgh. I arrived with the shirt on my back and that was about all. Finances were tight and my needs were many.

Our home was to be used extensively in the ministry, but the living room was bare except for a davenport in front of the window. So my wife, a young minister named Ken Smith, and I decided to pray for the specific needs of our living room. We prayed for two end tables, a coffee table, and a chair for the corner.

The next day the phone rang. A man asked for Ken and said,

"Rev. Smith, I don't know if you remember me or not, but you witnessed to me downtown the other day. Well, I'm being transferred to Buffalo, New York, where I've got a job sandblasting. I've arranged to dispose of most of my furniture, but there are some pieces I just can't get rid of. I hope you won't be offended, but I got to thinking maybe you could use them. Could you find any use for two end tables, a coffee table, and a corner chair?"

Ken dropped the phone. He picked it up and answered the man that we'd be right over. We rented a trailer, and by that afternoon the room was furnished.

We lived on the north side of town, and it was difficult to get to the university on the east side. I spent eight hours a day on campus witnessing to students and really needed a car. Ray Joseph, a young seminary student, and I were meeting regularly at 5 A.M. on Wednesdays to pray about our lives and ministries. One morning we prayed specifically that God would provide a car to get me to campus.

The following Wednesday night the phone rang. It was a lady from First Presbyterian Church, who taught a class of adults. She said that one of the men in the class, Bill Newton, was getting a new car. The offer on the trade-in was so small that he wanted to give it to someone in need. Their class had heard I was working at the university and wondered if I could use a car. I told her that as a matter of fact I had been praying for a car.

She said, "Your prayers are answered!"

Bill and Edie Newton not only gave us the car, but also the whole class pitched in $125 to get the motor fixed, buy insurance for the year, secure the license plates, and to top it all off gave us $50 for gasoline.

I had moved to Pittsburgh from the West Coast and soon discovered that my clothing was a bit out of style at this prestigious Eastern school. The students wore dark grey single-breasted suits, black and grey neckties, and black shoes and socks. Each Monday night we ate dinner in a different fraternity house and presented the Gospel. In the midst of this sea of black I stood out like a Roman candle. I had a light green double-breasted suit, a colorful, flowered necktie, and a pair of yellow crepe-soled shoes. So I began to pray about my wardrobe. Within a week God provided a dark suit that fit perfectly. The following week Ken Smith and I were helping an elderly lady in his church with some chores around her house. As we finished the job and were walking out, she stuffed a paper sack under my arm. On the way home I opened the sack and discovered a pair of black shoes that fit perfectly.

Another need I had was a watch. Mine had been broken that summer by some kids in a Vacation Bible School I had led in my hometown of Neola, Iowa. Because I had no watch, I was occasionally late for appointments and knew that this dishonored the Lord. So I prayed.

One night I spoke to the Saturday Night Bible Class that had been started through the ministry of Dr. Donald G. Barnhouse. The following Wednesday night a member of that class came to our house with a thank-you gift. It was a box about the size of *Halley's Bible Handbook,* and I was delighted. But when I opened it, I discovered it was not a handbook but a wristwatch, an Omega Automatic that I still have. To me as a young Christian leader in a strange city, God showed over and over again that He was ready, willing, and able to provide for my needs.

Faith also means that we *believe that what we do for God will prosper.* "He is like a tree planted by streams of water, which yields its fruit in season and whose leaf does not wither. Whatever he does prospers" (Ps. 1:3).

Our property has a creek running through it—a creek surrounded by weeds, trees, and wild flowers. My wife's garden, her pride and joy, is back there as well. She cares for it constantly. When a plant looks unhealthy, she nurtures it back to health with water and plant food or fertilizer. However, she does not crawl down into the creek to care for the trees and bushes that are growing wild. Her eye is constantly on the things *she* has planted. The Bible teaches that we are not wild plants growing here and there. We are "trees planted" by our Heavenly Father. We are under His constant care and protection, surrounded by the rivers of His love, mercy, and grace.

The psalmist emphasizes this truth again: "He will not let

your foot slip—He who watches over you will not slumber; indeed, He who watches over Israel will neither slumber nor sleep. The Lord watches over you—the Lord is your shade at your right hand" (Ps. 121:3-5).

Recently I read of an incident in the life of a famous sea captain during the days of the great sailing vessels. He was crossing the Atlantic from Liverpool to New York when the ship ran into a fierce storm. The waves were gigantic, the wind blew with hurricane force, and the ship was violently tossed about.

The passengers were terror-stricken, pulling on their life vests and preparing for the worst. The captain's eight-year-old daughter was aboard that trip. She was awakened by the noise and cried out in alarm asking what was wrong. They told her of the storm and the perilous condition of the ship.

She asked, "Is my father on deck?"

They assured her that he was.

She smiled, laid her head back on her pillow, and was asleep in minutes.

This is the kind of childlike faith that pleases God. He assures us that He keeps our souls, that He never slumbers nor sleeps.

Faith further means that we *believe God to be absolutely trustworthy.* This was illustrated once by my youngest son. He had outgrown his little bike and wanted a bigger one. We went down to the bike shop and looked them all over. He didn't nag and whine when we discussed whether we could afford one or not. His attitude was "Whatever you think is best, Dad."

"Righteous are You, O Lord, and Your laws are right. The statutes You have laid down are righteous; they are fully trustworthy" (Ps. 119:137-138). God has never done a single wrong thing. What He calls upon us to believe and do is absolutely right. His Word is utterly trustworthy. What He decides, where He leads, and what He says is right. His promises are sure. His will is good, acceptable, and perfect.

In addition to relying on the promises, protection, and trustworthiness of God, we can observe another beam shining from the character of God and related to faith: *God's power.* This summer I was meditating on the story of the father and child as recorded in Mark 9. Jesus and three of the disciples had come from the Mount of Transfiguration to find a discouraging scene. The father had brought the child to Jesus' disciples for help, but they were unable to do any good. Jesus asked the father how long the condition had existed.

The father answered, "from childhood" (v. 21). He continued, "It has often thrown him into fire or water to kill him. But if You can do anything, take pity on us and help us" (v. 22). Notice the word *anything*. The father would have been satisfied with any sort of help.

But Jesus answered, " 'If you can?' said Jesus. 'Everything is possible for him who believes' " (Mark 9:23).

His answer is fascinating. The father had said, "If You can." Jesus answered, "Everything is possible for him who believes." The father says "anything"; Jesus answered, "everything." The problem is never what or how much Jesus can do. The problem rests in what we can believe. As Jesus told two blind men on another occasion. "According to your faith will it be done to you" (Matt. 9:29).

The inner life of leaders will either make them or break them. If they neglect the cultivation of purity, humility, and faith, they are in for big trouble. On the other hand, if they set themselves to be God's kind of people, "The eyes of the Lord [will] range throughout the earth to strengthen those whose hearts are fully committed to Him" (2 Chron. 16:9). By God's grace you can be such a leader.

Chapter Four

The Leader's Attitude toward Others

As the previous chapter explains, the outward performance and success of Christian leaders depend for the most part on their inner life. No person who is self-serving, proud, lazy, or hypocritical *should* have followers. We will now look at the inner life of leaders in another area: their basic attitudes toward others.

The Apostle Paul said, "The goal of this command is love, which comes from a pure heart and a good conscience and a sincere faith" (1 Tim. 1:5). The ultimate objective of all of his instruction was to produce love toward others, a good conscience in themselves, and true faith in God. This is the basis of a life of joy. J–O–Y: Jesus first, Others second, and Yourself last.

Let's look at the crucial inner characteristics that will most enhance the leader's relationships with those who follow.

A Servant Heart

Jesus gave us the basic summary of His life: "For even the Son of Man did not come to be served, but to serve, and to give His life as a ransom for many" (Mark 10:45). He was among us as One who served (see Luke 22:27).

Today it is not possible for us to serve the Lord by taking a sacrificial animal to the side of a hill, kindling a fire, and presenting it to Him. To serve God we must serve others, as Jesus did. Leaders must offer their own lives on the altar of God to be consumed in the flame of God's love, in service to others. "This is how we know what love is: Jesus Christ laid down His life for us. And we ought to lay down our lives for our brothers" (1 John 3:16).

This, of course, is contrary to the practice of most secular leadership. Go into any business office where the organizational chart of the firm is displayed, and you will see that the leader has his or her name at the top with lines running from top to bottom. And in most cases that leader and the higher echelons of management demand service from others.

Jesus came and reversed the direction of service without giving up His leadership. He told His apostles:

> Jesus called them together and said, "You know that the rulers of the Gentiles lord it over them, and their high officials exercise authority over them. Not so with you. Instead, whoever wants to become great among you must be your servant, and whoever wants to be first must be your slave—just as the Son of Man did not come to be served, but to serve, and to give His life as a ransom for many" (Matt. 20:25-28).

Much of the teaching of Christ was revolutionary and strange to the hearers of His day. His teaching regarding leadership continues to have an unfamiliar ring in an age that calls for us to climb to the top. The Bible teaches that to lead is to serve. In our more spiritual moments we recognize the truth of this concept and respond with a warm, positive attitude. The problem, however, arises in the day-to-day doing of it. It is so much easier to let the other person bring the iced tea on a hot muggy day. How long has it been since we've shined somebody's shoes for him or her—to say nothing of washing that person's feet!

One evening my wife and I served a fish dinner to about twenty men. Some of the guys had been to the lake and returned with about forty beautiful rainbow trout. We topped the meal off with gallons of homemade ice cream. After we had eaten our fill, one of the fellows suggested they help with the clean up. Great idea!

As the men organized themselves into furniture straighteners, floor cleaners, garbage haulers, and dishwashers, I saw a sight that was hard to believe. One of the fellows who had eaten the most and enjoyed it to the fullest got up from his chair, walked over to the window, and hid behind the drapes. That's right! *He hid behind the drapes!*

After the work was organized and well underway, he stepped out, moved to a chair, sat down, and began to read a magazine. Remember the statement of Jesus, "I am among you as One who serves" (Luke 22:27). This fellow had it turned around.

There is always room for one more servant. The small areas in the spotlight can get a bit crowded, but there is always room in the shadows for the person who is eager to serve.

Stephen was a man full of faith and power, and the enemies of Christ were not able to resist the wisdom and the spirit by which he spoke. He had a remarkable grasp of the Word of God and the boldness to preach it with conviction. One day the apostles came to him and asked if he would serve tables for some Grecian widows who were being neglected in the daily distribution of food.

Stephen could have said, "Me? Serve tables? Apparently you are unaware of my wisdom, power, faith, and preaching ability. Get someone else to stand in the shadows and serve. I'm sure you can see that I am better suited to the spotlight in center stage."

But no, thank God, that was not his reaction. He eagerly took his place among the six other servants and waited on tables. I'm sure that is one of the prime reasons he has held a place in God's spotlight down through the centuries. Only one person could be the first martyr in the cause of Christ and Stephen was it. No one can ever replace him.

The Bible teaches that the way up is down. "The greatest among you will be your servant. For whoever exalts himself will be humbled, and whoever humbles himself will be exalted" (Matt. 23:11-12).

A Sensitive Spirit

A second necessary attitude of the leader toward others might be described as a sensitive spirit. Jesus again is our best example of this. Observe His reaction to people's needs.

During those days another large crowd gathered. Since they had nothing to eat, Jesus called His disciples to Him and said, "I have compassion for these people; they have already been with Me three days and have nothing to eat. If I send them home hungry, they will collapse on the way, because some of them have come a long distance" (Mark 8:1-3).

Jesus knew how long a person could go without food. He had fasted forty days and nights in the wilderness. But He didn't look around at the multitude and insist that they gather for another meeting. He could have told them, "Don't talk to Me about hunger. I know what hunger is. I went for forty days without food, and these people have only been out here for three days. Tell them to stop complaining. We have just begun."

This is a common failing among people in leadership positions. They evaluate their own capacities and expect everybody else to keep up with them. But that's not the way it is. Many sincere Christians who have warm hearts toward the Lord are limited in their abilities. They need a slightly slower pace and a shorter distance. Because leaders can work harder longer, have a greater capacity for prayer, and more intense hunger for the Word, they can usually outdistance those around them. That's what makes them leaders.

So leaders must be sensitive to the needs of the people and compassionate in their dealings with them. One thing they must do above all else: get to know them as individuals.

One day my son came home from school. I told him about my day and how things had gone. Then he began to tell me about his. He mentioned how much he liked a certain teacher. So I asked him why.

It was simple. "Dad, he knows my name." Amazing! It had nothing to do with the man's ability or background. He didn't say whether the man was loud or quiet, gentle or tough. The teacher knew Randy's name. That's all.

But the Lord spoke to me through that situation. People hunger to be recognized. Not only that, if leaders are worth their salt, they must get to know them. It is the only way they can do them any good or lead meaningfully.

The Scriptures clearly teach that we must deal with people according to their individual characteristics. "And we urge you, brothers, warn those who are idle, encourage the timid, help the weak, be patient with everyone" (1 Thes. 5:14).

Three types of people are mentioned in this passage. The first are those who need to be held in line — the *unruly*.

A shepherd would certainly understand this aspect of leadership, spending his days in keeping the foolish sheep from hurting themselves or going astray. "He chose David His servant and took him from the sheep pens; from tending the sheep He brought him to be the shepherd of His people Jacob, of Israel His inheritance. And David shepherded them with integrity of heart; with skillful hands he led them" (Ps. 78:70-72).

Perhaps the "unruly" includes those who when faced with a problem or difficulty want to throw in the towel and quit. They could go on, but they find it easier not to. Possibly they were offended by someone and want to pick up their marbles and go home. This, of course, is the reaction of people who are immature. They have to be handled with kid gloves. The reason? They are kids. But they do need to be helped, and the leader must stick with them. It requires an overload of patience and earnest prayer, but it can be done.

The second group mentioned are the *feebleminded,* or, better, the fainthearted, the timid. These are the people who tend to be afraid of their own shadows. They need to be led to the place where they are able to take a step of faith, and eventually launch out into the deep and experience the trustworthiness of God.

The greatest help to these people is to hear testimonies of others who have been over the road and who have found the Lord faithful. God can use these testimonies to build courage into the lives of the timid.

Some years ago a Bible study for women met in our city, led by Mrs. Morena Downing. Morena has walked with the Lord for many years and her radiant testimony and deep faith in God have been an inspiration to many — including me. Her class had grown quite large and scores of women testified that it was through Morena's leadership that they had sort of "come out of their shell."

Many now feel confident in witnessing. Others are bold in their stand for righteousness and truth, even when such a stand is not popular. As a result, numerous people have met the Savior through the lives of these women. Morena has truly strengthened the "fainthearted."

Harvey Oslund is a Christian leader in our nation's capital whose life has been mightily blessed of God. Today many men and women who have been reached and trained by this man are serving the Lord around the world. One of his strengths is the ability to inspire people to give sacrificially to God.

Again, it is not so much what Harvey says but he what he is. His life, his money, all that he has and is has been given to God. He is one of the most generous men I have ever met. I have talked to people who have learned the joy of giving because of his example. Before they met Harv, they were afraid to give; they sat on their billfolds while hesitantly putting a small coin in the collection plate. Seeing Harv's life changed all that for them. Today their lives are marked by sacrifice and generosity. When special needs come along, they dig deep, take bold steps of faith, and experience the joys of giving.

Remember "It is more blessed to give than to receive" (Acts 20:35). Timid, hesitant, reluctant nongivers have become bold, joyful givers. How? Once "fainthearted," they were challenged by the life of a man who was setting the pace. His life and testimony inspired them, strengthened them, and enabled them to change.

The last group mentioned are people who are *weak*. I believe this refers to believers who are plagued by besetting sins. The instruction is "Help the weak." Here again are people who need special attention, often personal, individual help. Quite frequently they are most helped by the opportunity to talk over their weaknesses with someone they trust, and who they know will keep the conversation in confidence. It is a frightening thing to hear a story you shared with your leader repeated to the whole group, even though the names have been changed to protect the guilty!

The fact that a Christian has a lingering battle with a sin that plagues him or her is certainly no indication that he or she lacks potential usefulness to the Lord. Dawson Trotman, founder of The Navigators, often told of his battle with profanity as a young Christian. He would determine to stop, only to fail again and again. Eventually, through the patient love and fervent prayers of a godly Sunday School teacher, he was able to overcome the habit by the help of the Lord.

Rod Sargent is a man mightily used of God throughout the world today. As a young Christian, however, he experienced many difficulties because of his alcoholism. Before his conversion he spent many a night in Los Angeles bars, only to wake up next morning with splitting headaches followed by terrifying blackouts. He came to Christ through a Christian fellowship in Pasadena, and continued to meet with the group for Bible study and prayer. But he would occasionally succumb to the old temptation to go to a bar for a few drinks.

This double life brought on the fear that the group would find out and no longer welcome him. The leader of the group, however, knew what was going on, but continued to meet with Rod for prayer and fellowship in the Word. He practiced the scriptural admonition, "Help the weak." Today Rod is himself a respected Christian leader. The man who had helped him had a sensitive spirit, knew Rod's need, and met it.

Get to know the people you would lead. Know those who need to have a fire built under them to get them moving and those who need to be held back. Some have great talents and need to put them to work. Others are prone to tackle things that are a bit beyond their abilities and capacities. If allowed to plunge ahead, they will likely find themselves over their heads in responsibilities and demands that are beyond them.

These two things, then, a servant heart and a sensitive spirit, are crucial for a good leader. If you are to lead, these characteristics must be an integral part of your life. "So give Your servant a discerning heart to govern Your people and to distinguish between right and wrong. For who is able to govern this great people of Yours?" (1 Kings 3:9)

Chapter Five

Why Some Leaders Excel

The good is the enemy of the best. Too often when people are asked about a class or a series of meetings or a calling program, they reply, "Oh, it was OK." Some may say, "It was terrible!" This is almost a consolation, for all too often responses seem to fall into that bland ground of mediocrity. Satisfaction with the status quo shows that a program is really in trouble. This is especially true when a leader knows there is apathy and is content to have it so.

On the other hand, some programs stand out visibly. They are fresh and alive, and the people involved are enthusiastic, motivated, and productive. Looking behind the scenes, you find a leader who has qualities not found in the average person. He or she is a leader who excels.

Excellence

The first necessary quality in leaders who stand out is the spirit of excellence. They who strive for excellence will not be counted among the also-rans. But where do people start in an effort to develop this attribute? How do leaders develop a spirit of excellence in a day when almost anything can be passed off as good enough? The answer: they must start with God Himself. They must consider the excellence of God and His attributes.

• *God's name is excellent.* "O Lord, our Lord, how majestic is Your name in all the earth! You have set Your glory above the heavens" (Ps. 8:1). "Let them praise the name of the Lord, for His name alone is exalted; His splendor is above the earth and the heavens" (Ps. 148:13).

• *God's loving-kindness is excellent.* "How priceless is Your unfailing love! Both high and low among men find refuge in the shadow of Your wings" (Ps. 36:7).

• *God's greatness is excellent.* "Praise the Lord. Praise God in His Sanctuary; praise Him in His mighty heavens" (Ps. 150:1).

• *God's salvation is excellent.*

"Surely God is my salvation; I will trust and not be afraid. The Lord, the Lord, is my strength and my song; He has become my salvation." With joy you will draw water from the wells of salvation. In that day you will say: "Give thanks to the Lord, call on His name; make known among the nations what He has done, and proclaim that His name is exalted. Sing to the Lord, for He has done glorious things; let this be known to all the world" (Isa. 12:2-5).

• *God's work is excellent.* "Listen, O heavens, and I will speak; hear, O earth, the words of my mouth. . . . I will proclaim the name of the Lord. Oh, praise the greatness of our God! He is the Rock, His works are perfect, and all His ways are just" (Deut. 32:1-4).

• *God's way is excellent.* "As for God, His way is perfect; The Word of the Lord is flawless. He is a shield for all who take refuge in Him" (2 Sam. 22:31).

• *God's will is excellent.*

Therefore, I urge you, brothers, in view of God's mercy, to offer your bodies as living sacrifices, holy and pleasing to God—this is your spiritual act of worship. Do not conform any longer to the pattern of this world, but be transformed by the renewing of your mind. Then you will be able to test and approve what God's will is—His good, pleasing and perfect will (Rom. 12:1-2).

Many other Scriptures also carry this theme. Note this carefully: a spirit of excellence in the life of a leader is a reflection of one of God's attributes. Too often Christians misunderstand this emphasis and associate it with fleshly effort and worldly ambitions. This is not so! Throughout the Scriptures we observe a constant emphasis on emulating God, being like Him.

David, toward the end of his life, made an interesting statement regarding the work of building the temple.

David said, "My son Solomon is young and inexperienced and the house to be built for the Lord should be of great magnificence and fame and splendor in the sight of all the nations. Therefore, I will make preparations for it." So David made extensive preparations before his death (1 Chron. 22:5).

Why did David feel so strongly about this and insist that the temple of God must be of great magnificence? Because it reflected on the name of God, which is excellent in all the earth. This Scripture is a pointed reminder to the leader: if what you are doing is in the name of the Lord, make certain it reflects well on that name, that it is exceedingly magnificent.

The desire to do things with excellence is Christlike. It was said of Him, "He has done everything well" (Mark 7:37). It is amazing to observe Christian leaders who emulate the compassion and love of Christ but completely miss this aspect of His character. I have seen sermon topics such as "Becoming More Like Jesus" in church bulletins so sloppily done that they were a scandal and a disgrace. What a paradox!

I remember hearing John Crawford who for years represented The Navigators in New Zealand tell about a construction job he was heading up in Los Angeles. The Navigators were constructing their new office building. It was almost completed, and the crew was working on the back door that led into the alley. Dawson Trotman was due to return to Los Angeles shortly, and they were rushing to complete the job before he came home.

Trotman, the founder of The Navigators, was a man of exacting standards. So the work on the office had been done with that in mind. However, since there was hardly any traffic by the back door, and because they were in a hurry, they finished it with halfway measures.

When Dawson returned, he was enthusiastic about the way the office looked. He inspected everything and was full of compliments for the workers. Then he saw the back door. "John," he said, "we'll have to change that door."

"But, Daws, it only leads to the alley."

"Yes, I know, John," Daws answered, "but when we do things for the Lord, the back door must look just as good as the front."

I've often thought about that statement and wondered what motivated Daws to think that way. I suppose it's because he knew that God sees the back door in the same way He sees the front, even if a person does not.

Dawson's secretaries tell of his exacting standards on how envelopes and letters had to look. Pastors around the country wrote to tell them how they had been challenged by the appearance of the letters from The Navigators. Some even mentioned the care with which they now prepared the church bulletins, greatly raising the standards of their appearance.

During summer conferences at Glen Eyrie, the international headquarters of The Navigators, I have sometimes asked people at the end of a busy week, "What was the biggest challenge you've had from your time here?" More often than not the answers have been:

"The diligence with which the young men mop these floors!" / "I was amazed at the way you keep the grounds." / "I was really challenged by the way those guys washed windows in the castle."

The influence of one man who insisted on things being done with excellence remains long after his death.

In the Parable of the Talents, the good servant is commended; the slothful servant is not only denounced, but his sloth is equated with wickedness (see Matt. 25:14-30). Recall also Paul's admonition: "Never be lacking in zeal, but keep your spiritual fervor, serving the Lord" (Rom. 12:11).

God works in our lives in at least seven ways to bring about the spirit of excellence.

1. By helping us realize our own weakness. "But He said to me, 'My grace is sufficient for you, for My power is made perfect in weakness' " (2 Cor. 12:9).

2. Through the prayers of others. "Epaphras, who is one of you and a servant of Christ Jesus, sends greetings. He is always wrestling in prayer for you, that you may stand firm in all the will of God, mature and fully assured" (Col. 4:12).

3. Through someone sharing the Word with us. "Night and day we pray most earnestly that we may see you again and supply what is lacking in your faith" (1 Thes. 3:10).

4. As we study the Bible for ourselves. "All Scripture is God-breathed and is useful for teaching, rebuking, correcting, and training in righteousness, so that the man of God may be thoroughly equipped for every good work" (2 Tim. 3:16-17).

5. Through suffering. "And the God of all grace, who called you to His eternal glory in Christ, after you have suffered a little while, will Himself restore you and make you strong, firm, and steadfast" (1 Peter 5:10).

6. By giving us a hunger for holiness. "Since we have these promises, dear friends, let us purify ourselves from everything that contaminates body and spirit, perfecting holiness out of reverence for God" (2 Cor. 7:1).

7. Through a desire to have the fruit of our lives brought to perfection. "The seed that fell among thorns stands for those who hear, but as they go on their way they are choked by life's worries, riches, and pleasures, and they do not mature" (Luke 8:14).

Some words of caution need to be sounded at this point. First, we need to examine our motivation. Excellence for its own sake is not our standard, but excellence for Christ's sake.

I have been married for many years to a wonderful woman. To my shame I must admit that at times I have forgotten our wedding anniversary. But when I've remembered it, I have brought my wife roses. Now, how would it be if I marched into our home on June 21 and said, "Well, here they are! More roses! For years I have brought these things to you, and here is another bunch. Right on time. I feel it is my duty to do this, so here they are! Enjoy them!"

How would that go over? Like a cement zeppelin! If I bring roses simply because on anniversaries I bring roses, they mean little.

Now let's say it's one of those years when I fail to remember. Three days later it hits me like a helicopter blade that our anniversary has come and gone. I hurry down to the florist and get a bunch of roses and walk into the house with them held behind my back. I go up to Virginia and say, "Well, Sweetheart, I'm sure you know what I did. It baffles me how you can manage to put up with the likes of me, but I'm glad you do. Sweetheart, I want to give you these roses, tell you I love you madly, and ask your forgiveness. Can you find it in your heart to forgive me one more time?"

Let me ask you, how does that go over? Like a new bike at Christmas! Why? I wasn't on time, I had forgotten, I had blown it. In the first instance I was right on time doing the right thing, but it didn't count. In the second instance I had failed, but all turned out well. Why? Motivation made the difference.

The second thing to bear in mind is that there has been only one Person who has ever lived *who did all things well*. That Person, of course, was Jesus. With that in mind, read carefully Hebrews 13:20-21 (KJV): "Now the God of peace, that brought again from the dead our Lord Jesus, that great shepherd of the sheep, through the blood of the everlasting covenant, make you perfect in every work to do His will, working in you that which is wellpleasing in His sight, through Jesus Christ, to whom be glory for ever and ever." The writer sets quite a standard—"Make you perfect in every good work to do His will!"

How can anybody possibly achieve that? "Through Jesus Christ!" Through Jesus Christ, the only One who has ever done all things well, every moment of every hour of every day of His life. So my only hope of achieving a Christlike standard of excellence is to completely relax in the arms of Jesus and let Him live His life through me. No amount of sweat and strain can accomplish it. No amount of self-effort and high resolves. Only "through Jesus Christ" can this be obtained.

He who is the Author and Finisher of our faith waits to take over our frustrations and failures and turn them into joyful accomplishments that bring glory to the Lord. The One who still does all things well is waiting to "make you perfect in every good work . . . working in you that which is wellpleasing" to God.

Initiative

The second characteristic of the successful leader is initiative. Leaders don't wait for things to happen; they help make things happen. They're out at the point of the action. That's one reason some people shy away from leadership responsibilities. They know that "they who would lead the band must face the music." One of the necessary traits of leaders is that they be willing to do just that.

The Scriptures abound with examples of people who took the initiative in accomplishing God's purposes in their day. For example, David chose Joab to be his general for this very reason. "David had said, 'Whoever leads the attack on the Jebusites will become commander-in-chief.' Joab son of Zeruiah went up first, and so he received the command" (1 Chron. 11:6). Isaiah also stepped out from the ranks to become a voice for God in his generation. "Then I heard the voice of the Lord saying, 'Whom shall I send? And who will go for Us?' And I said, 'Here am I. Send me!' " (Isa. 6:8)

It is obvious that initiative is a basic quality of leadership. Suppose there is a giant snowstorm the night of the midweek prayer meeting. A few hardy souls make it to church, open the doors, turn on the lights, and wait for the pastor to arrive. Unknown to them, however, the pastor is stalled in a snow drift and is working furiously to get his car moving again. He borrows a shovel and digs out. He hails a couple of guys to give him a push but all to no avail. His car doesn't budge, and the time is getting later and later.

Meanwhile, back at the church the people are wondering what's happened to their pastor and are sitting around waiting for church to begin. Finally one of them stands up and suggests that they sing a hymn or two while they wait. He announces the page and begins to lead the song. In this example it doesn't matter whether the man has ever led music or not; he has become the leader. He may be skillful or not. He may or may not know anything about how to go about it. By the simple act of exercising a little initiative in standing to his feet, he has become the leader. He may do a good job or a bad one, but regardless of his performance, he is the man in charge. Initiative is one of the major responsibilities of leadership.

Of course, all Christians should take initiative in presenting themselves to God for service. Bible characters who never became known particularly as leaders were richly blessed and used of God simply because they served spontaneously.

Rebekah became the wife of Isaac and "the mother of millions" because she took the initiative in serving Abraham's steward. She volunteered to draw water from the well, not or him but also for his camels, a big chore; and this act arked her as God's chosen bride for Isaac (see Gen. 24:14-21).

A small boy became the focal point of a great miracle because he stepped forward and offered his lunch to help feed a hungry multitude (see John 6:9-11).

But the greatest example in Scripture is God Himself. "Simeon has described to us how God at first showed His concern by taking from the Gentiles a people for Himself" (Acts 15:14). Left to themselves the Gentiles would not have come to Him.

So the Lord took the initiative. "But God demonstrates His own love for us in this: While we were still sinners, Christ died for us" (Rom. 5:8). To take the initiative is a Godlike characteristic.

Leaders must be alert to exercise initiative in many ways. One, already suggested, is in the area of serving. The Apostle Paul demonstrates this vividly. The ship in which he was traveling to Rome was wrecked on the island of Melita. "The islanders showed us unusual kindness. They built a fire and welcomed us all because it was raining and cold. Paul gathered a pile of brushwood and, as he put it on the fire, a viper, driven out by the heat, fastened itself on his hand" (Acts 28:2-3). Here is Paul, an older man, gathering firewood for the others. No doubt he was as tired as the rest, but he took the initiative to serve the others, as Christ would have done when He walked the earth.

The leader of a teenage Bible class in our city, a young man named Mark Sulcer, gave of himself unreservedly. He hauled the teens around in his car to various church and school functions. He straightened up after them following the Bible classes. Mark was always available to them day or night. I could see that these kids had not met anyone quite like him before and were much impressed.

When Christmas came, two teens got their heads together and planned to get Mark a surprise present. Without telling anyone about it, they went to a shopping center and made all the arrangements. When Christmas Eve came, they gave Mark his present. He opened the box to find a silver trophy cup with the engraving: "To the world's second greatest servant."

Mark's life and example rubbed off on his followers, and they are showing signs of growth in this area. His initiative is paying dividends.

A second way of exercising initiative is to take the first step toward reconciliation. Two Scriptures give clear guidance in this area. "Therefore, if you are offering your gift at the altar and there remember that your brother has something against you, leave your gift there in front of the altar. First go and be reconciled to your brother; then come and offer your gift"

(Matt. 5:23-24). "If your brother sins against you, go and show his fault, just between the two of you. If he listens to you, you have won your brother over" (Matt. 18:15). If you have offended a Christian brother or sister and the Lord brings this to mind, you should take the initiative to go and ask for his or her forgiveness. If, on the other hand, a person has offended you, you should still take the initiative to go to that person and talk it over and get it straightened out. In either situation, *it's your move first!*

This, of course, is one of the hardest things in the world to do. It is especially difficult for a leader. Several missionaries have told me of struggles they have had with this while on the field. Pride was the chief obstacle. When they were willing to swallow their pride and take the initiative, the Lord brought joy, deliverance, and blessing into their respective situations.

One of the devil's tactics is to make leaders think that if they humble themselves and go to a member of the group to ask for forgiveness or get something straightened out, the person will look down on them. Nothing could be further from the truth. It is in that very act that leaders are at their best, and the other person knows it. Usually a leader will win a loyal follower, a good friend, and faithful helper in the work.

A third area in which to exercise initiative is that of seeking knowledge. "The purposes of a man's heart are deep waters, but a man of understanding draws them out" (Prov. 20:5). The joy of the leader is complex, and he or she cannot be expected to know all there is to know about everything. Therefore, a leader should seek out knowledgeable Christians and learn from them.

Again, pride often gets in the way. I recall an incident in my own life when this happened. I had been transferred from a ministry in the field to a responsibility at headquarters. I had not spent a great deal of time at our home base prior to this, and so was not too sure about what went on. I found myself on committees discussing things about which I knew very little. But I was hesitant to admit this and ask questions. I thought they expected me to be knowledgeable. I was convinced that to start asking questions would reveal how ignorant I was. So I continued in my ignorance.

From time to time, for example, I would be invited to sit with the finance committee. Months passed before I discovered that when they referred to the I.R.S., they were talking about the income tax people! You can imagine how valuable I must have been to this committee. Had I forgotten my pride and taken the initiative to ask some questions, I might have been of some service. Leaders cannot afford to behave as I did. They must actively seek the information they need to carry on their work properly. They must ask questions. They must be willing to learn from others.

Initiative is defined as *the spirit needed to originate action.* How does a leader acquire that spirit? How does one become the sort of person who originates actions? The most productive thing a leader can do is *to train himself or herself to think ahead.* A leader has been described as a person who sees more than others see, who sees further than others see, and who sees before others do.

If leaders train themselves to think ahead, it will have two positive effects on their work. *First, it will help keep them out of trouble.* They will avoid snares and pitfalls down the road. They can ask themselves, "If we do this, what is likely to happen? In turn, what will that lead to? When that takes place, will it lead to this result? Do we want that result? If not, let's not even start in that direction." *Second, by thinking ahead leaders can set goals* for themselves and their group. They can then think through the best ways to achieve those goals and begin to initiate actions along those lines.

All of this presupposes that leaders are in vital daily fellowship with the Lord through the Word and prayer (see chap. 2). Otherwise, they may be led by their own understanding or set up plans using the wisdom of the world as their guide. Leaders must remember that truth is found in Jesus Christ. Secular management books or textbooks on leadership are helpful, but our basic resource is God. "For the foolishness of God is wiser than man's wisdom, and the weakness of God is stronger than man's strength" (1 Cor. 1:25).

Creativity

The third reason some leaders excel is that they are creative. They are not afraid to try new and different things. When you look at the lives of the apostles, you do not find the monotony and stiffness that characterizes so many lives today. This difference may be traced to the very nature of God as contrasted to human nature.

To explain, God is a God of variety and order, while people thrive on conformity and disorder. People struggle to conform. Go into any city, look at the houses made during the same period of time, and they all look alike. People fight to be like others in speech, dress, and that which they buy. Music can be identified with the various decades; it has a sameness about it.

How refreshing it is, by contrast, to see the Lord at work! He loves variety. I am astounded by the diversity in a zoo. The alligator, giraffe, and elephant reveal God's love for variety. The flowers and birds and trees teach the same truth. Scientists tell us that no two snowflakes are alike. When we reflect on all of this, isn't it sad that our work for God is so different from the work done by Him. The same old dull, bland programs are carried on year after year. Creativity, generally, is sadly lacking.

The creativity of the Lord was demonstrated to me in an astounding, remarkable, and humorous way. My wife and I were visiting Soviet Russia. As we made ready to depart, we were required to sign a paper declaring we were taking no Russian rubles out of the country. We were allowed to keep the small change for souvenirs, but it was a crime, subject to severe punishment, to try to leave the country with Russian paper money. We exchanged the rubles we had for American dollars, and signed the paper. We cleared the passport check and waited in the lounge for the plane to take us to Helsinki.

Our plane was eventually called, and we lined up to be searched. The first man through was a very large, loud American tourist. After they had checked his carry-on luggage, he passed the metal detector, and the bell rang. He emptied his pockets and tried again. The bell rang. He took off his belt and tried again. Bong! By this time he was becoming quite amused by it all and started to laugh. He could be heard all over the waiting room. This happened over and over again with the same result, and he laughed louder and louder.

Here were about forty of us waiting to have our handbags, purses, and carry-on luggage searched, and a fat, loud American, stripped down to a pair of tight-fitting pants and T-shirt was going round and round through the metal detector and continually ringing the gong. There was absolutely no reason for the bell to ring, but it did. The guard grew more agitated, and the crowd became more hilarious all the time. We were at an impasse.

Through all this commotion, my wife was standing next in line waiting to have her purse searched, not knowing that at the bottom were eight Russian rubles! She had missed them when we exchanged the money. She was all set to be caught and convicted of a serious crime in Russia. But the show went on. The man kept ringing the bell while he roared with laughter. The plane departure was delayed, but the crowd didn't mind. They had never seen anything like it. It was a carnival. But it was not funny to the guard. One of the gods of the Soviet Union is their technology, and their god was being mocked by a crowd of American tourists.

Finally the guard, angry and frustrated, screamed, "Go!" My wife innocently walked to the plane carrying her forbidden rubles. When we arrived in Helsinki, she discovered the money, and we were shocked. Then we knew why the bell had rung for no apparent reason. The Lord looked down, saw two of His foolish children in a jam, and got them out of it. Once again He displayed His innovative, creative nature. Creativity is part of His being.

Sometime ago I was sitting in the office of the president of an international Christian organization. We were discussing the work of God around the world, and he showed me a letter he had just received from one of his field workers. The letter was full of news and contained many encouraging reports of God's blessing on the work. But one sentence was highly disturbing to the leader. It said, "We've been following the same program for the past five years, and it's still producing."

The president looked up at me and said, "If they have been following that same program for the last five years, it's obvious they shouldn't be. There must be a better way!"

I've given a lot of thought to that statement, and I'm con- vinced he is right. There *must* be a better way! Surely we haven't hit on the best possible approach to reaching the lost or discipling believers. Surely there is room for improvement. Surely God can reveal changes and new approaches that will reap a greater harvest for His kingdom.

The creativity of four nameless men who brought their friend to Jesus has long been a challenge to me.

> So many gathered that there was no room left. . . . Some men came, bringing to Him a paralytic, carried by four of them. Since they could not get him to Jesus because of the crowd, they made an opening in the roof above Jesus and, after digging through it, lowered the mat the paralyzed man was lying on. When Jesus saw their faith, He said to the paralytic, "Son, your sins are forgiven" (Mark 2:2-5).

Here were four men who had a problem. They had a friend they wanted to bring to Jesus but found it to be seemingly impossible. The record says, "They could not get him to Jesus." No way. They could have said, "Sorry, friend. We tried but we just can't do it." But they didn't. Their compassion and love for the man and their zeal to get him to Jesus led to a bold and creative plan. They would tear a hole in the roof and let him down from the top. Can't you just see the reaction? "You can't do that! That's never been done before! You will disrupt the service. Someone is liable to get hurt by a falling tile." But they did it, and the Holy Spirit faithfully recorded it for our instruction.

How do you gain a creative spirit? One way is to keep yourself in the proper frame of mind. Constantly be on the lookout for a better way. Train yourself to think, "If it works, it will soon be obsolete." Maintain an open and probing mind. Pray for the boldness and courage it will take to try something new when God reveals it to you.

But the main thing is to live in constant, close, intimate fellowship with Jesus Christ. He is creative. "For by Him all things were created: things in heaven and on earth, visible and invisible, whether thrones or powers or rulers or authorities; all things were created by Him and for Him" (Col. 1:16). Everything in the invisible spiritual world was created by Jesus Christ. Everything in the visible physical world was created by Him. That's why the Bible speaks of Christ as the One by whom God "made the worlds" (Heb. 1:2, kjv). Worlds. Plural: visible and invisible. Do you want to be a creative person? Then you must invest much time in fellowship with the One who is the most creative Person in the universe.

When He walked the earth as a doer-teacher, Jesus astounded those who met Him. What He *did* was different. What He *said* was different. They were astonished at His doctrine. " 'No one ever spoke the way this man does,' the guards declared" (John 7:46). Some complained that He lived contrary to their longstanding traditions. You and I look back and say, "Thank God, He did!"

By the same token, you and I must be willing to break new ground and step out of the established mold. When the Lord sees leaders in His work with this spirit and desire, He can place His hand on their lives and say as He did of old, "Behold, I will do a new thing!"

Three things, then, we must seek from the Lord. One is a sense of excellence. The means for achieving excellence, once we've made it our standard, is to relax in the arms of Jesus and let Him live His life through us. He's the only One who "did all things well." The second is initiative. Here again the Lord Himself is our greatest example. To learn from Him as we seek to do His work is the most productive path we can follow. Third is a creative spirit. Again, openhearted fellowship with Jesus Himself is the best means of seeing creativity developed in our lives by the Spirit of God.

Chapter Six

How to
Make an Impact

His father was a mess. When you look at the record of the father, King Ahaz, you begin to wonder if all he did was sit around thinking up new ways to sin and lead the people astray. For sixteen years he wallowed in the mire of wickedness. He made molten images to pagan gods and burnt his children in the fire after the way of the heathen. He closed the doors of the house of God and set up idolatrous altars on every corner in Jerusalem. After he had blown it for sixteen years, he died.

As was the custom of the time, his son reigned in his stead. When Hezekiah took over the kingdom, he was 25 years old. He had seen what his father's sins and corruption had done, and he wanted no part of it. He was determined to change things and call the nation back to God. When we consider the mess he inherited, we might conclude that very little could be done in one man's lifetime, but we would be wrong. In a very short time the situation was completely reversed. "There was great joy in Jerusalem, for since the days of Solomon son of David king of Israel there had been nothing like this in Jerusalem" (2 Chron. 30:26).

It's an amazing story. Hezekiah made an impact for God that was truly marvelous. As you study his life, you see that it is characterized by a few basic principles. Three are readily identifiable.

Wholeheartedness

The first principle in making an impact for God is wholeheartedness. "In everything that he undertook in the service of God's temple and in obedience to the law and the commands, he sought his God and worked wholeheartedly. And so he prospered" (2 Chron. 31:21).

The Apostle Paul exhorts us along similar lines, "Whatever you do, work at it with all your heart, as working for the Lord, not for men" (Col. 3:23). Solomon put it this way, "Whatever your hand finds to do, do it with all your might, for in the grave, where you are going, there is neither working nor planning nor knowledge nor wisdom" (Ecc. 9:10). As we read these passages, we can see that God wants people who are eager and zealous. But what do we find to be the spirit of the age in which we live? Are we frequently exhorted to wholeheartedness? Hardly. Almost daily we hear people telling us, "Take it easy" / "Don't work too hard" / "Don't overdo it." The dangerous thing is that this lack of wholeheartedness can be picked up by Christian leaders. When it is, it spells mediocrity and failure in their work.

My high school ideal was a senior nicknamed "H-ball." He excelled in sports and was a good student. I would imitate his walk and mannerisms. I learned to dribble a basketball like he did and shoot the same way. He pitched on the baseball team, and I copied everything he did, including the way he wore his cap. I was determined to become the pitcher when he graduated.

The year following his graduation I showed up for baseball tryouts. The coach came over to me and asked if I'd like to play. "Would I? Coach, I'll give it all I've got. I want to play so bad I can feel it."

In every way I knew, I tried to communicate to him my eagerness and determination. He was pleased and told me to suit up and see what I could do. I made the team. In fact, I became the pitcher.

What do you think would have happened if I had told the coach, "Oh, I don't know. I've been giving it some thought, but it's no big deal. Maybe I'll try out for the team, but it's not all that exciting to me." Why, the coach wouldn't have given me a second look. That would have been the end of my baseball career.

Do you think God has lower standards than my high school baseball coach? Not at all! God is looking for people who make wholehearted commitments to Him and to His service. The soft, slovenly, half-hearted spirit of the age is not His standard. But it is hard to keep a biblical standard in an undisciplined age. Your standard of performance must be high.

In my first year of Christian service in the Midwest, I met a young man named Johnny Sackett. We began to fellowship together in the Word and prayer, and the Lord knit our hearts together. Johnny began to show great promise in the work of Christ. One day he asked me if he could join our team. I explained to him what was involved, and he was eager to be part of our gang. He was a great colaborer, full of dedication and enthusiasm.

For a number of months things went great. One weekend we planned a team activity of witnessing on the campus of Iowa State University. When it came time to drive over to the school, I noticed Johnny was missing. When I inquired about it, one of the guys told me he had decided not to go. When I asked if he was under pressure of studies or didn't feel good or had some responsibilities with his parents, I was told that he just decided not to go.

We went without Johnny and had a fruitful time. We met quite a few students who were eager to talk about the Lord, and some committed their lives to Him. We returned full of joy and thanksgiving to God.

On Monday I borrowed a friend's VW and drove down to see Johnny. After we had talked awhile, I asked if he had understood the standards the team had set for itself. He said yes, and he was happy to be a part. I told him that because I enjoyed having him on the team, I was sorry he had chosen not to work with us anymore. He was shocked and asked what I meant. I reminded him that one of our standards involved being available when we had a ministry together. He began to sob. After he regained his composure, he got out of the car and went to his room.

I prayed for Johnny daily for about two weeks and then got a letter from him. He thanked me for making it mean something to be part of the ministry and then gave me thirteen reasons why he should be included. I immediately telephoned him and joyfully welcomed him back. He became one of our most productive men then and has served the Lord on two continents since. The problem had been that he had no idea that I really meant it when I talked about standards of commitment and wholeheartedness. Sympathy for him could have let the incident slide, but compassion would not.

When Jesus said, "If any man will come after Me, let him deny himself and take up his cross daily, and follow Me," He meant it. Frankly, as I look back at this incident over the years that have passed, I know I would handle the situation differently today. I would be quicker to show the tenderness and gentleness of Christ. But the principle remains inviolate.

My drill instructor in Marine boot camp insisted on high standards of performance, not because he was trying to be mean to me, but because he knew I was going to war, and he had to instill habits into me that could save my life. He was not doing me harm. He was doing me good. And when I was under fire, and death and destruction were all around me, I was grateful for all that I had learned. By the same token, leaders must manifest the spirit of wholeheartedness so that those who follow them will have their hearts in the work. Had Hezekiah displayed anything less than wholehearted involvement, the nation could not have turned from its sins in such a remarkable fashion. It was his leadership that showed the way and set the tone for the behavior of others.

I was in Minneapolis working out on weights with a friend of mine named Bill Cole. Another fellow joined us for a while, and as he was leaving the gym, I had 185 pounds over my head in a bench press. He looked at me and said, "Take it easy!" Had I taken it easy at that moment I would have killed myself! Naturally he wasn't intending that; it was just his way of saying good-bye. But I've thought about that often. Even when it doesn't fit and would be the death of the person if he followed that advice, we still say, "Take it easy!" Frankly, I don't need that sort of exhortation. I am prone to do that without any outside help. My undisciplined, slovenly, lazy nature tells me to do that all the time. What I need is to be challenged to hit it with all I've got.

Leaders must consider the following fact. They are not only building for the present but also for the future. If their hearts are lukewarm, what will the future hold? What will the people they have trained be like? Will their hearts burn with whole-hearted zeal for God? Not if the leaders' hearts are lukewarm, for only fire kindles fire. When Jesus cleansed the temple, His actions reminded the apostles of the Old Testament Scripture, "Zeal for Your house will consume Me" (John 2:17; see Ps. 119:139). Both passages speak of being consumed with zeal for God. When was the last time you reminded anyone of a Scripture that spoke of being devoured with holy zeal? Is an eager and ardent spirit as out of date as the horse and buggy? Are cheerleaders at high school sports events the only ones left in our society who enter into their jobs with zeal and gusto? A truly Christlike leader will demonstrate the same fire and intensity that Jesus displayed.

Wholeheartedness and zeal are the outgrowths of a love that burns in the leader's heart. From there it spreads to the hearts and lives of others, who catch the flame of that spirit. Some feel that leaders should play it "cool" lest they frighten off some people. This is not so. If the leader plays an adult game, then adults will come to play. The first commandment is still in the book: "Hear, O Israel, the Lord our God, the Lord is One. Love the Lord your God with all your heart and with all your soul and with all your mind and with all your strength" (Mark 12:29-30).

Singlemindedness

The second thing to observe in the life of Hezekiah was his singlemindedness. He got right at the main job and stuck with it.

> In the first month of the first year of his reign, he opened the doors of the temple of the Lord and re-

paired them. He brought in the priests and the Levites, assembled them in the square on the east side and said: "Listen to me, Levites! Consecrate yourselves now and consecrate the temple of the Lord, the God of your fathers. Remove all defilement from the sanctuary" (2 Chron. 29:3-5).

He was not sidetracked, either by overwhelming odds, ridicule, or opposition.

Three biblical writers give us reasons for singlemindedness. Peter says, "But the day of the Lord will come like a thief. The heavens will disappear with a roar; the elements will be destroyed by fire, and the earth and everything in it will be laid bare" (2 Peter 3:10). *Everything in this world is temporal and transient.* Two things transcend this world and will last throughout eternity: the Word of God and people's souls. When leaders give themselves to these, they are locked on eternal values. The things of the world clamor for their attention, but they keep their eyes single to the things that last.

A second reason for being singleminded is suggested by the words of James: "Why, you do not even know what will happen tomorrow. What is your life? You are a mist that appears for a little while and then vanishes" (James 4:14). *Life is too short to be wasted.* When people see this truth, it helps them remain on track despite the incessant bombardment of the world seeking to turn them aside, to get their eyes off Jesus. The Word of God tells us where to look:

> Therefore, since we are surrounded by such a great cloud of witnesses, let us throw off everything that hinders and the sin that so easily entangles, and let us run with perseverance the race marked out for us. Let us fix our eyes on Jesus, the author and perfecter of our faith, who for the joy set before Him endured the cross, scorning its shame, and sat down at the right hand of the throne of God (Heb. 12:1-2).

The third reason for singlemindedness is stated by Paul, "Therefore, my dear brothers, stand firm. Let nothing move you. Always give yourselves fully to the work of the Lord, because you know that your labor in the Lord is not in vain" (1 Cor. 15:58). When we are following the straight and narrow path with our eyes on Jesus, we have the assurance that what we are doing is worth something. What a thrill it is for leaders to know that while multitudes are throwing their lives away in worthless activities, their service for Christ counts for eternity.

The Bible is filled with examples of people who were single-minded in their walk with God. Moses is typical.

> By faith Moses, when he had grown up, refused to be known as the son of Pharaoh's daughter. He chose to be mistreated along with the people of God rather than to enjoy the pleasures of sin for a short time. He regarded disgrace for the sake of Christ as of greater value than the treasures of Egypt, because he was looking ahead to his reward (Heb. 11:24-26).

The Apostle Paul sounds the same note, "Brothers, I do not consider myself yet to have taken hold of it. But one thing I do: Forgetting what is behind and straining toward what is ahead, I press on toward the goal to win the prize for which God has called me heavenward in Christ Jesus" (Phil. 3:13-14).

But the greatest example is Jesus Himself. "As the time approached for Him to be taken up to heaven, Jesus resolutely set out for Jerusalem" (Luke 9:51). His disciples saw this and were amazed. "They were on their way up to Jerusalem, with Jesus leading the way, and the disciples were astonished, while those who followed were afraid. Again He took the Twelve aside and told them what was going to happen to Him" (Mark 10:32). Why were they amazed? Because He knew exactly what awaited Him and marched forward without flinching. " 'We are going up to Jerusalem,' He said, 'and the Son of Man will be betrayed to the chief priests and teachers of the law. They will condemn Him to death and will hand Him over to the Gentiles' " (Mark 10:33).

Something in Jesus' countenance caused the Twelve to feel uneasy. They were afraid of what lay before them and were awed by the courage of their Leader. Jesus Christ went with unfaltering steps straight to the cross. He knew His mission and He was set to fulfill it. So it must be with us. The world nags at us to become ensnared with this or encumbered with that, but the Word of God calls us to strip down, lay aside every weight, and press toward the mark. Singlemindedness is not easy, but it is necessary.

When Billy Graham preached Dawson Trotman's funeral sermon, he spoke of Daws' singlemindedness. He told us, "Here was a man who did not say, 'These forty things I dabble at,' but 'This one thing I do.' "

A person can destroy his or her life in one of three ways. The first is to give in to a lazy slothful nature and do nothing. I've seen young people go down that road. They buy a guitar, put on a pair of cutoffs, go to the beaches of sunny California, and waste their lives lying around frying in their own fat.

The second way to destroy your life is to give yourself to a goal, work hard, and discover at the end that you gave yourself to the wrong goal. I have known many who have done this. Some have poured out their story in bitter regret and tears.

The third way is what Dr. Graham was talking about. Become a dabbler and never really do anything.

Joshua was warned about dabbling: "Be strong and very courageous. Be careful to obey all the law My servant Moses gave you; do not turn from it to the right or to the left, that you may be successful wherever you go" (Josh. 1:7). This is not a warning against walking down the wrong path, but against turning first to one side and then another.

I've watched people like that. They start out well, but something comes along that grabs their fancy and they are sidetracked. They finally see the folly of their ways and turn back to the path, only to be sidetracked again by something else farther down the road. A pitiful thing! Good people, with good hearts, going nowhere. Why? Easily diverted. The singlemindedness of Moses or Paul or Christ Himself is not a part of their lives.

Someone complains, "That's tough to do." Of course it's tough! The Apostle Paul said, "I *press* toward the mark." He did not say, "I float toward the mark, I glide toward the mark, I slip and slide toward the mark, or I drift toward the mark." He said *press,* and that always presupposes opposition. The world will lure you, and the devil will fight you, but if you run the race looking toward Jesus, He will enable you to finish well.

Paul's testimony vividly illustrates this: "However, I consider my life worth nothing to me, if only I may finish the race and complete the task the Lord Jesus has given me—the task of testifying to the gospel of God's grace" (Acts 20:24). He speaks of "the race." The greatest joy in life is to know that you are in the perfect will of God, doing what He wants in the way He wants it done.

The warriors of Zebulun challenge us in this regard: "Men of Zebulun, experienced soldiers prepared for battle with every type of weapon, to help David with undivided loyalty—50,000" (1 Chron. 12:33). Here were men that went into battle, trained, equipped, disciplined, and singleminded.

Each of us has a course to follow, a mission to accomplish, a goal to attain, "Tell Archippus: 'See to it that you complete the work you have received in the Lord' " (Col. 4:17).

I recall an incident in my life that determined my destiny. My wife and I had met the Lord through reading the Bible. We did not have many people around us who could give us deep spiritual counsel, but we both became convinced we should follow the Lord with singleness of purpose. A pastor, the Rev. Arlan Halverson of Harlan, Iowa, told us about a school in Minneapolis where we could learn the Word of God. We were new Christians and eager to grow. So we determined to go to that school and give our lives completely to Christ's service. I had a good job at the time, and when I began to tell my co-workers about what I was planning to do, I received nothing but static. They called it foolishness—fanaticism. Throwing away a good job with high pay and security was madness. But we knew what we must do.

I quit my job and prepared to leave Council Bluffs, Iowa, for Northwestern College. We sold some of our possessions, gave away most of the rest, and were free to go. We put our clothing and a few household items in small boxes, loaded them on a child's coaster wagon, and headed for the train station. Virginia pulled the wagon and I pushed, and we launched out on a road of high adventure. We determined we would not only not look back, but also we would not even look to the right or to the left. We would keep our eyes on Jesus and follow Him wherever He led. Many years have passed and we have faced opposition and trials, but He continues to show us the way.

Today the Lord is looking for people who care nothing for the empty praise or temporal pleasures of this world. He is seeking men and women who care that the world needs Christ and who are eager to follow Him with singlemindedness and purpose. The testimony of Paul is an encouragement:

> For I am already being poured out like a drink offering, and the time has come for my departure. I have fought the good fight, I have finished the race, I have kept the faith. Now there is in store for me the crown of righteousness, which the Lord, the righteous Judge, will award to me on that day — and not only to me, but also to all who have longed for His appearing (2 Tim. 4:6-8).

A Fighting Spirit

In addition to his wholehearted and singleminded approach to the job, Hezekiah also demonstrated a remarkable fighting spirit. In spite of unbelievable odds, he pressed ahead with enthusiasm and faith. His messengers were mocked by some as they went from place to place. "The couriers went from town to town in Ephraim and Manasseh, as far as Zebulun, but the people scorned and ridiculed them" (2 Chron. 30:10). Did it slow down his work? Not at all. "This is what Hezekiah did throughout Judah, doing what was good and right and faithful before the Lord his God" (31:20).

This is the basic spirit we see in the lives of God's leaders throughout the Bible. Paul's testimony is:

> Five times I received from the Jews the forty lashes minus one. Three times I was beaten with rods, once I

was stoned, three times I was shipwrecked, I spent a night and a day in the open sea, I have been constantly on the move. I have been in danger from rivers, in danger from bandits, in danger from my own countrymen, in danger from Gentiles; in danger in the city, in danger in the country, in danger at sea; and in danger from false brothers. I have labored and toiled and have often gone without sleep; I have known hunger and thirst and have often gone without food; I have been cold and naked. Besides everything else, I face daily the pressure of my concern for all the churches (2 Cor. 11:24-28).

What was Paul's attitude through all his difficulties? "For it has been granted to you on behalf of Christ not only to believe on Him, but also to suffer for Him" (Phil. 1:29).

Nehemiah faced continual opposition from the enemy.

But when Sanballat, Tobiah, the Arabs, the Ammonites and the men of Ashdod heard that the repairs to Jerusalem's walls had gone ahead and that the gaps were being closed, they were very angry. They all plotted together to come and fight against Jerusalem and stir up trouble against it (Neh. 4:7-8).

His fighting spirit is revealed in his response: "But we prayed to our God and posted a guard day and night to meet this threat" (v. 9).

Time and again the opposition mounted an attack to keep Nehemiah from accomplishing his objective, and every time he prevailed.

Sanballat and Geshem sent me this message: "Come, let us meet together in one of the villages on the plain of Ono." But they were scheming to harm me; so I sent messengers to them with this reply: "I am carrying on a great project and cannot go down. Why should the work stop while I leave it and go down to you?" Four times they sent me the same message, and each time I gave them the same answer (6:2-4).

The Apostle Paul calls our attention to the life of a soldier, an athlete, and a farmer.

> Endure hardship with us like a good soldier of Christ Jesus. No one serving as a soldier gets involved in civilian affairs — he wants to please his commanding officer. Similarly, if anyone competes as an athlete, he does not receive the victor's crown unless he competes according to the rules. The hardworking farmer should be the first to receive a share of the crops (2 Tim. 2:3-6).

The mark of a good soldier is that he or she worries the enemy. The enemies of the cross of Christ became nervous when Paul was around. Because of his work in Ephesus, Demetrius the silversmith was convinced all was lost (see Acts 19:23-28). Paul was opposed by the leaders of false religions and the demons of hell, but he was undaunted. He truly demonstrated the mark of a good soldier.

Athletes compete with opponents, of course, but quite often their main competition is with themselves. They have to overcome their own doubts and fears, their sloth, and the desire to pamper themselves. The Apostle Paul tells of the battle in his own life.

> Everyone who competes in the games goes into strict training. They do it to get a crown that will not last; but we do it to get a crown that will last forever. Therefore I do not run like a man running aimlessly; I do not fight like a man beating the air. No, I beat my body and make it my slave so that after I have preached to others, I myself will not be disqualified for the prize (1 Cor. 9:25-27).

Leaders will constantly face problems and difficulties from others but often their main battles are with themselves.

The farmer faces droughts, floods, and pestilence of every variety. I recall how some in Iowa suffered a tremendous hailstorm a few years ago. The corn had been about six feet high but was so badly hit that you could hardly tell it was a cornfield. The storm was so violent that it knocked the steeple off the church and broke countless windows. A seed company in Shenandoah, Iowa, heard of our plight and sent some help. They brought a truckload of soybeans and told us if we would get them in the ground, we would have feed for the livestock for the winter.

We didn't know much about soybeans in those days, but we knew it was too late to replant the corn. So we gave it a try. Sure enough, we were able to get enough feed for the animals to make it through the winter. The storm was a tremendous blow to my brother who was running the farm, but to this day I can see him rolling up his sleeves and fighting back. I'm sure it would have been easy for him to throw up his hands and cry, "What's the use?" But he didn't. He demonstrated the true fighting spirit.

After Waldron Scott and his family went to the Middle East as missionaries in the late 1950s, everything went wrong. Finances were so low that they couldn't afford furniture. So Joan made a slipcover for their steamer trunk, and they sat on it in the living room. The water heater blew up and burned her quite severely. Through a series of strange circumstances, Scotty was thrown in jail. They literally were pressed to their knees. Only the fighting spirit of this family and their faith in the promises of God kept them going. Today there are young men and women throughout the Middle East whose lives were touched with the Gospel of Christ that Scotty and Joan subsequently shared with them. These Christians are strong, rugged soldiers of the cross who saw a clear example of a true soldier of Christ. Out of impossible circumstances came a harvest for the kingdom.

This is what made the servants of Christ in the new Testament church so outstanding. They had the fighting spirit of committed warriors for God. They were men and women "who have risked their lives for the name of our Lord Jesus Christ" (Acts 15:26). Does this characterize the leadership of the Christian enterprise today? In some cases, yes, but all too often we look at a person's intellectual powers or their educational achievements as the apex of all good. I heard a man praised on one occasion because he had a ten thousand-volume library! Obviously there is nothing wrong with owning or reading good books. We are to love the Lord our God with all our *minds.* But leaders must never stop there. It is not a brilliant mind but a fighting spirit that will keep them going when all semblance of order has crumbled around them.

Early in his Christian life, the Apostle Paul was shown what he was to suffer. "But the Lord said to Ananias, 'Go! This man is My chosen instrument to carry My name before the Gentiles and their kings and before the people of Israel. I will show him how much he must suffer for My name' " (Acts 9:15-16). He was shown the prize he was to gain, but he was also shown the price. He knew the cost of discipleship. Later he said, "May I never boast except in the cross of our Lord Jesus Christ, through which the world has been crucified to me, and I to the world. . . . Finally, let no one cause me trouble, for I bear on my body the marks of Jesus" (Gal. 6:14, 17). When the apostle wanted to refute his detractors, he showed them the scars on his back. The early Christians faced dangers, whips, and lions. They were heroes in the true sense of the term. We face push buttons, television, and foam rubber. May God give us the same fortitude and faith men and women of God have always shown.

These three things, then, are essential to making an impact as a leader. We must be wholehearted, singleminded, and have a fighting spirit. Programs may continue without these, but leaders whose lives are to be used of God to produce much lasting fruit will see that they have all three.

Chapter Seven

Setting the Stage for Success

Plan a Good Beginning

Beginning is difficult. You're new to the job; the people around you are watching to see what you will do; and you may feel uneasy and insecure. Some people in that situation cover their feelings of inadequacy by beginning to "bull their way around." This normally upsets people, and you spend the next few months trying to get out of the hole.

Lorne Sanny told about a lesson he learned while he was running a military service center in Southern California. When he first took the job, he would stand in front of the center, hand out invitation cards to military people passing by, and ask them to come in. Most walked right on by. Then he hit on an idea. He would go up the street a few blocks and fall in step with some guys who were walking along. He would get in a conversation with one or two of them, and when they got to the center, he'd ask if they wanted to stop in for a cup of coffee and talk for a while. More often than not some of them would take him up on it.

When we begin a new job, we must not try to stop people and try to get them to abruptly change directions. We must fall in step with them for a while and walk along in the direction they are heading. Then, after we have established a little communication with them, we can suggest a change of direction. That way we are more likely to have a hearing and get a positive response.

The Bible gives us some guidance in this matter in a rather strange setting. Saul is not known as a model of spiritual leadership. His failings and shortcomings have often been noted by preachers in the pulpit and by authors of books. But I am challenged by the good beginning this man had as a leader — and by the wisdom he showed. We can learn an important lesson from his example.

Samuel had called the people together unto the Lord to Mizpeh. From the tribe of Benjamin, Saul was taken. "But when they looked for him, he was not to be found. So they inquired further of the Lord, 'Has the man come here yet?' And the Lord said, 'Yes, he has hidden himself among the baggage' " (1 Sam. 10:21-22). It is obvious that Saul was not seeking the job or trying to put himself forward. He displayed great restraint and control over his own spirit when some of the people mocked him. "But some troublemakers said, 'How can this fellow save us?' They despised him and brought him no gifts. But Saul kept silent" (1 Sam. 10:27).

Sometime later a situation arose that required a bold step of leadership. The Ammonites wanted to put out their right eyes and make servants of the people of Javesh, or else they would make war on them. To submit would have rendered the people of Javesh helpless to protect themselves. In warfare, a large shield blocked much of the vision of the left eye; hence, to lose the right eye was to be severely handicapped in battle. They could still tend sheep and plant crops, but their ability to defend themselves would be lost.

Meanwhile, Saul had returned to his farm and was tending his sheep. To me that fact speaks volumes about the man. Here was a man who had been anointed king of Israel, but he was not immediately trying to throw his weight around. He was back with the sheep. No doubt he was waiting for some situation to arise in which he could be of genuine help to the people. He was waiting until his new responsibility matched a real need. In such a case, the people would appreciate his leadership and be glad to follow him.

The Ammonite threat was that kind of situation. When Saul heard of the plight of his people, he sent out a call to muster the troops to come to the aid of those in need. The people came with one consent. In the ensuing battle, Saul's forces devastated the Ammonites.

After the people were delivered from their oppressors, they were so committed to Saul that they thought to make retaliation against the men who had mocked him earlier. "The people then said to Samuel, 'Who was it that asked, "Shall Saul reign over?" Bring these men to us and we will put them to death' " (11:12). Saul immediately stepped in. "No one shall be put to death today, for this day the Lord has rescued Israel" (v. 13).

Notice, Saul did not call attention to himself by saying, "I have done this or that," but he gave all the glory to God for what had been accomplished.

At this point Saul had Israel's full allegiance and confidence. The people were ready to follow him. He was off to a good start. His call from God was evident to all. His actions and bold step of faith had wrought deliverance for the downtrodden.

This is a great lesson for anyone who has been called to lead. Don't be in a hurry to make a lot of changes. Don't be in a hurry to show anybody who's boss. If you have some changes you would like to set in motion, first just get people thinking in that direction.

This is another lesson I have learned from Lorne Sanny. He usually saw things before the rest of us Navigators. So he would begin to plant seed thoughts. He would toss out an idea or ask a question that would get us thinking along certain lines. Then when the plan was actually proposed, some of us had been thinking about it so long that we thought it was our idea!

Changes can be made. New ideas will be adopted. New directions can be instituted. But it often takes time. People resist change. So fall in step with them, walk with them in their direction for a while, and then gradually ease them into new and more productive paths.

Do Your Homework

After you're off to a good beginning, there is another thing you must practice. Do your homework. Become known as the person who has the answers. When you have a project to propose or a suggestion to make, know the facts. Know what it will cost. Know how long it will take. Be able to explain why it is a good idea.

The Book of Nehemiah is often studied by leaders. Nehemiah—the ancient governor of Jerusalem—is frequently called the effective executive. Here was a man who knew how to get things done. Let's take a look at him in action to see what we can learn about doing our homework.

Nehemiah had been living in the comfort of the palace, holding the prestigious position of cupbearer to the king. One day he learned of the desperate plight of his people in Jerusalem: "They said to me, 'Those who survived the exile and are back in the province are in great trouble and disgrace. The wall of Jerusalem is broken down, and its gates have been burned with fire' " (Neh. 1:3).

The Lord burdened Nehemiah's heart with this news, and it sent him to prayer (see v. 4). One day, some time later, he was going about his duties but still burdened in his heart for the situation in Jerusalem. The king noticed his depressed mood and asked him, "Why does your face look so sad when you are not ill? This can be nothing but sadness of heart" (2:2).

Upon then hearing of Nehemiah's concern, the king asked, "What is it you want?" (v. 4) The first thing Nehemiah did was to pray to the Lord, and then he gave the king his answer. And his answer is classic. He had done his homework. If he hadn't, he would have stumbled around and quite possibly blown his opportunity.

Nehemiah said,

> "If it pleases the king and if your servant has found favor in his sight, let him send me to the city in Judah where my fathers are buried so that I can rebuild it."
>
> Then the king, with the queen sitting beside him, asked me, "How long will your journey take, and when will you get back?" It pleased the king to send me; so I set a time. I also said to him, "If it pleases the king, may I have letters to the governors of Trans-

Euphrates, so that they will provide me safe-conduct until I arrive in Judah? And may I have a letter to Asaph, keeper of the king's forest, so he will give me timber to make beams for the gates of the citadel by the temple and for the city wall and for the residence I will occupy?" And because the gracious hand of my God was upon me, the king granted my requests (vv. 5-8).

I hope you will catch the significance of that little scene. From what we saw earlier, it is obvious that Nehemiah had been on his knees before God and had spent much time in prayer over the problem. But he didn't stop there. He had thought through what he would need to do the job. It is obvious he thought in terms of an answer to his prayers. And he was ready when the answer came.

Imagine what would have happened when the king asked him what he needed, if he had said, "Well, O King, I haven't thought much about it. I'd kind of like to go out there myself, with your permission, of course, and I suppose I'd need some favors from you. Could I go and think about it for a few days?"

But no! Nehemiah had done his homework and knew exactly what the project demanded: letters to the governors beyond the river; a letter to the keeper of the king's forest; soldiers and some horsemen. He had done his homework.

Plan the Work

When you are given a responsibility, one of the first things you should do is spend time discovering exactly what your new mission is. Let me suggest that it generally breaks down into two distinct but related goals. One is to do something through the work to advance the cause of Christ. The other is to see that each member of your group have his or her life deepened in the Lord and become a more productive member of the body of Christ.

Let's discuss first how to accomplish your objective of forwarding the cause of Christ through the work. This can take the form of setting a goal to evangelize the area where your churc is located, getting a Gospel tract to every home in the city, and so on. You must then break this goal down into workable units and find qualified people to fill the key spots. Give them the authority to take action and check on them from time to time to make sure they are at the main job.

In our work we follow a four-step plan called **POLE:** Plan, Organize, Lead, and Evaluate. This can all sound cold and technical unless you think of it in an actual setting. Let's say, for instance, that some Saturday you and your group have decided to spend the morning cleaning up around the church. That is your goal. It's a nice day in early spring, and there is much to be done after a rather hard winter.

You decide to meet at 9 A.M. and work until noon. You ask members of the group to bring rakes, buckets, cleaning rags, paint brushes, brooms, mops, and whatever else you will need to get the job done.

You assemble, have a time of prayer, and commit your work to the Lord. Then you break the job down into workable units. Joe takes a couple of people and begins to work on the lawn. Pete and Hank start washing the windows. You and four others tackle the basement, cleaning and doing a little touch-up here and there with the paint brush.

Joe comes in about an hour later and says the lawn work is going well—raking, trimming the bushes, and so on, and wonders if they should go down to the nursery and get some flowers to set out. You go out and see how it is coming. It is immediately evident to you that if they start that additional project, they will not get the main job wrapped up by noon, namely, the cleanup project. So you suggest they stay with the original idea and then, if they get finished in time, take on the additional job of planting a few flowers. Joe is content with that suggestion and returns to the cleanup.

Now there are a couple of other ways you might have handled Joe. One would have been to read him off for getting sidetracked and tell him to follow orders and do what he was told. This would have accomplished two things: First, you would have taken the heart out of Joe for the job. Second, you would have stifled any idea sharing on Joe's part in the future.

Later, when you were trying to figure the best way to evangelize the neighborhood, Joe would have been afraid to speak up
for fear of being blasted out of the saddle.

Along about 11 A.M. you make the rounds to see how the
projects are coming. It is evident to you that Pete and Hank
are not going to get all the windows washed and that your own
crew is going to finish ahead of time. So you pull two guys
from your own crew and get them to help the window wash-
ers. At noon you assemble and take a look at what got done.
Mission accomplished. The tools are gathered and cleaned.
You have a word of prayer together to thank the Lord for the
good morning, hop in your cars, and head for home.

Any job will fit into that framework. You must think it
through and make a plan. Then you must organize it so that
every member of the group knows what his or her job is and
who he or she reports to. Then the leader must lead. Leaders
must set the example. They must roll up their sleeves and get
into the action. A periodic evaluation may lead to a midcourse
correction. At the finish of the job, it is good to sit down and
evaluate the whole project to see where things could have
been improved. This leads to better planning for the future.

Now let's take two of these points and look at them a bit
more carefully: selection of key people and your own involvement as a leader.

First, selection. The best painter is not always the best
person to head the paint crew. The one who heads the project
should be able to paint, but in addition he should be the sort of
person who inspires others to do their best and keeps the
spirit of the group high.

Before Jesus chose His twelve apostles, He prayed all night
(see Luke 6:12-13). The Apostle Paul told Timothy, "And the
things you have heard me say in the presence of many witnesses entrust to reliable men who will also be qualified to
teach others" (2 Tim. 2:2). He was to look for faithful people
with some ability to teach.

One thing I look for is when a person begins to call the
activity of the group "our work." It is evidence that this
person has gotten involved. When a new person joins a group,

he or she is somewhat of a spectator—watching what is going on. After some time he or she may begin to participate a bit more. Your goal is to lead this person from a spectator to a participant to one who is involved. It is from that last group that you want to look for your key people to head projects.

Make sure of your person before you give this person a key task. I've learned this the hard way. It is generally easier to get a person into a place of leadership than it is to get this person out. Paul said, "Do not be hasty in the laying on of hands" (1 Tim. 5:22). This refers to ordaining leaders, and it's good advice. Later on we'll take a look at some of the *qualities* to look for in selecting key people to help get a job done through the group.

Now about your own involvement in the work you lead. Should you roll up your sleeves and pitch in with the rest of the group? Absolutely! The power of example cannot be overstated. Peter told the leaders of the early church, "Be shepherds of God's flock that is under your care, serving as overseers—not because you must, but because you are willing, as God wants you to be; not greedy for money, but eager to serve; not lording it over those entrusted to you, but being examples to the flock" (1 Peter 5:2-3). We too should be "examples to," not "lords over." Christians have a Lord already.

Be involved in doing the work you expect to lead others to do. I once agreed to teach a Sunday School class for the summer. One of my goals was to increase the attendance of the class, which had been running at about twenty college-age kids, who came fairly regularly.

For the first two or three Sundays I encouraged them to bring someone to class the following week. No one did. So I began to make it a matter of prayer. During one of my prayer times the Lord revealed to me why no one was bringing anyone else to class: I wasn't.

I began to think how I could meet some college-age kids to bring to class. One Sunday I noticed a group of young servicemen lounging around the park next to the church, and the Lord gave me an idea.

The next Sunday my wife and I and our two kids went to

Sunday School a half hour early. We strolled over to the park and invited a few servicemen to come to Sunday School with us. Now there is nothing more harmless looking than a husband and wife and two kids. So some of them came. They had nothing else to do. When it came time to introduce the visitors, I'd introduce the three or four guys who came with me.

This went on for a couple of Sundays, and then one of the class members came and inquired where I was getting all these guys. I told him of my pre-Sunday School activity. He was interested and asked if he could come along. We met the next Sunday, split up to different parts of the park, and got quite a few guys. Some other members of the class caught the idea and began to do the same thing.

By the end of summer, scores of guys had met the Lord, and our class was averaging around 180 per week. I learned a simple lesson. My job was to teach the class and to provide leadership for them. It's summarized in Proverbs 4:11: "I guide you in the way of wisdom and lead you along straight paths."

In addition to seeing a mission accomplished through your group, there must also be a deep work done in the lives of each member of the group. The real test of your leadership is whether or not other leaders are developed as you lead the way. The development of Christlike character in the people for whom you are responsible is one of your prime objectives. Because of the importance of this point, it is discussed at length in chapter 11.

These have been a few tips—often learned the hard way—on how to begin your job and carry it out. I trust they will prove valuable to you as you grow in true spiritual leadership.

Chapter Eight

How to
Get More Done

It's a common problem. There's more to do than there is time to do it. The housewife, the worker, the boss, the student all face it. Projects to finish—tests to study for—reports overdue. The calendar and the clock: nag, nag, nag. If only I had more time.

Let me share a little secret with you that could change your life.

Do It Now

A simple idea is illustrated in the Book of Numbers in the Old Testament. We look in on the main character and what do we find? A busy man. Moses has been given the job of moving thousands of people out of slavery in Egypt across the burning sands of the Sinai to the Promised Land. And they are a troublesome bunch—always doing something stupid and incurring the disfavor of the Lord. Time and again God's patience is put to the test. And Moses is forever trying to straighten things out. He is constantly endeavoring to get across lessons in faith and duty and obedience and courage and purity of life. He is the leader of God's training program in the wilderness.

The people continually complain about lack of food or water, or the lack of variety in their menu. They murmur against Moses himself. They say the real reason he led them out of

Egypt is to kill them. Or he has married the wrong wife. Or all
this talk about God is just Moses' means of making himself a
big man. The problems seem endless. Moses has his hands
full.

And then one day out of the clear blue sky, the Lord drops
more work on him.

> The Lord spoke to Moses in the Tent of Meeting in
> the Desert of Sinai on the first day of the second
> month of the second year after the Israelites came out
> of Egypt. He said, "Take a census of the whole Israel-
> ite community. . . . You and Aaron are to number by
> their divisions all the men in Israel twenty years old or
> more who are able to serve in the army" (Num. 1:1-3).

Now, let's assume that Moses is human—like us. What
would your reaction have been? Mine would have been something like "Count everybody???!! Good grief, do You know
how long that will take? I've got my hands full now! Look at all
I'm doing: responsible for the physical and spiritual welfare of
all these people—that alone keeps me going from morning 'til
night—plus the fact that I *am* writing the Bible! I'm a busy
man with more to do than there's time for as it is. And now
I'm supposed to count everybody?"

Sound familiar? But hold on to your hat, and look at Moses'
response: "Moses and Aaron . . . called the whole community
together on the first day of the second month. The people
indicated their ancestry by their clans and families, and the
men twenty years old or more were listed by name, one by
one" (vv. 17-18).

Did you notice when the job was given? "On the first day of
the second month." And when did Moses start the project?
"On the first day of the second month." How about that!
There's a tremendous secret we can express in three words:
do it now. Especially if it is something that comes along while
you're doing something important.

I was in Oakland, California, on my way to speak to a group
of army men at Fort Ord. The chaplain had arranged for me to
share the Gospel with them. After that I was to go to another

part of town to speak at an "Andrew Dinner"—where some Christian men had invited their non-Christian friends to a pizza feed followed by a message. There was just one catch. In order for me to make both meetings, I'd have to miss supper. The schedule was that tight. Fine and dandy—no problem. But just as I was leaving the house a package came for me. It was a rather lengthy personnel form from headquarters that they needed right away. Bill already had the car started and in the driveway. What to do?

Take it with me and do it tomorrow? No time. Tomorrow we were heading for Hume Lake to visit a training program, and it would take the full day.

I called down for Bill to turn off the engine. I sat down and filled out the form. It took quite a while, but I got it done. I left it to be mailed, hopped into the car, and we made the meeting. Had I not done it then, I would have carried that thing around for days.

I am responsible for two categories of work: the kind I *like* to do and the kind I *have* to do. My tendency is to do what I like and leave until later what I have to do. The problem with that scheme is that the undone, unpleasant work is always pulling on my sleeve, reminding me it's there.

I really enjoy speaking to servicepeople about the love of God as revealed in Jesus Christ. It's a thrill to speak at an Andrew Dinner and watch the men lead their friends to Christ during the fellowship time that follows. Filling out personnel forms? *Blah!* I *could* have waited—and when the long-distance phone call came, I could have just given headquarters my schedule. They are reasonable people. They would probably have understood. But for the next week every time I reached into my briefcase for my Bible, there would have been that packet of papers, leering at me. And so I took the time to "do it now" and hit the road with a released spirit.

As you read the record of Moses' life, you don't get the idea that "paper shuffling" was his thing. But when God gave him a great long personnel form to fill out, rather than sit down and complain that he didn't have time—or that he was involved with something *really important*—or that "surely somebody else could take care of things like *that"*—he *did it now.*

You're probably thinking, "OK, fair enough. I can see how that would help in certain instances, but there's another problem. There's more to do than I can do by myself. I need some help."

Right. This situation faces us all from time to time. The Sunday School superintendent needs teachers. The pastor needs workers. The missionary needs personnel for his or her staff to help in the physical end of things. The sponsors of the young people's department need drivers of automobiles. The deacons need help in distributing food to the needy. The committee for the annual church dinner needs help. This problem is universal. It comes to all of us at one time or another.

Trust God for the Help You Need

As in so many situations in life, the Christian has an advantage here that the non-Christian knows nothing about. Again, this is illustrated in the life of one of the busiest characters in the Old Testament, Aaron.

When his appointment came, I suppose Aaron's reaction was about what ours would have been. Thankfulness, exhilaration, excitement, a sense of unworthiness, and gratitude for the privilege of being involved in such an important work. "Bring Aaron and his sons to the entrance to the Tent of Meeting and wash them with water. Then dress Aaron in the sacred garments, anoint him and consecrate him so he may serve Me as priest" (Ex. 40:12-13).

At first I suppose the tremendous significance of the job and the importance of the task occupied most of Aaron's working thoughts. What a position to hold! And think of the honor of having his sons serve beside him! Of all men he was truly blessed of God.

But as they got into the work, another train of thought must have been set in motion: *This is really a busy job in more ways than one! All these people continually bringing their offerings. All these cattle to be sacrificed to the Lord. And the tremendous job to keep the area cleaned up! Burning certain parts, saving certain parts, burying certain parts—work, work, work! What I need is help.*

No doubt the thought remained with Aaron for some time, and intensified when the two oldest sons, Nadab and Abihu, died before the Lord when they offered strange fire. Now he was left with only two sons, and the two youngest at that! The task that seemed great before must have seemed mountainous now. How in the world could he get all his work done?

The New Testament says, "And my God will meet all your needs according to His glorious riches in Christ Jesus" (Phil. 4:19). Aaron's need was help. And I'm sure he had no idea how he was going to get it. But God knew. He had a plan all along. He had 22,000 Levites waiting in the wings ready to go to work.

"The Lord said to Moses, 'Bring the tribe of Levi and present them to Aaron the priest to assist him' " (Num. 3:5-6).

So now, in addition to his two young sons, he had 22,000 men between the ages of thirty and fifty to help. Isn't that just like God! When God meets a need, He *meets* it!

A number of Scriptures tell us of the relationship the Lord intended Aaron to have with these men. Two of these contain vital lessons for us as we are given people to help us in our God-given tasks.

Numbers 8:11, 19:

> Aaron is to present the Levites before the Lord as a wave offering from the Israelites, so that they may be ready to do the work of the Lord. . . . Of all the Israelites, I have given the Levites as gifts to Aaron and his sons to do the work at the Tent of Meeting on behalf of the Israelites and to make atonement for them so that no plague will strike the Israelites when they go near the sanctuary.

The clauses, "Aaron is to present the Levites before the Lord," and "I have given the Levites as gifts to Aaron," teach an important truth. Here the Levites were offered by Aaron to God, and then God gave them back. This is to be true not only of helpers in our tasks but also of our homes, our professions, our children, and our very lives.

Numbers 18:6: "I Myself have selected your fellow Levites from among the Israelites as a gift to you, dedicated to the Lord to do the work at the Tent of Meeting."

Do you see the truth revealed in the words, "as a gift to you, dedicated to the Lord"? These helpers are a gift *from* the Lord *for* the Lord. Not for you but for God. And if He sees fit to use them in another capacity, in a new job, rejoice! You can't outgive God. Notice too that helpers in our tasks are gifts from God.

So the lesson in all this is faith. Trust the Lord. He has promised to supply and He will. But as in every other aspect of life, you must exercise faith. Believe God. And trust Him to provide the *right kind* of help.

In Aaron's case, God provided men between the ages of thirty and fifty. Here were men with good judgment and stability. When Moses was called upon to number the people, it was "All the Israelites twenty years old or more who were able to serve in Israel's army were counted according to their families. . . . The families of the tribe of Levi, however, were not counted along with the others" (1:45, 47). The Levites were called to a *spiritual* warfare.

Why were the Levites recruited to their tasks at the age of thirty, while the soldier was recruited at age twenty? Note a New Testament parallel. Qualifications for church officers include: "He must not be a recent convert, or he may become conceited and fall under the same judgment as the devil" (1 Tim. 3:6) and, "They must first be tested; and then if there is nothing against them, let them serve as deacons" (v. 10). The person engaged in spiritual work must not be a novice, and he must first be proved.

By the way, the Levites quit at age fifty—probably so they wouldn't run down at the end of their service! God gave Aaron tested, proven men who were alive and active to help him in his work and spiritual warfare.

Focus on Objectives, Not Obstacles

Want to get more done? Make your first rule "do it now." Second, trust God to supply the help you need. And there is a third thing. It has to do with the focus of our attention, or the way we look at things. Somehow we seem to be wired to think negatively. It is so easy to focus on all the problems involved in a task. People rather commonly expect the worst. Example: someone receives a telegram late at night.

"You open it."

"No, you open it."

They both expect it to contain bad news.

The phone rings in the night. What's your first thought — positive or negative?

Negative attitudes can carry over in our outlook toward a task we're involved in. It can make us problem-centered rather than goal-centered. We tend to look at the difficulties. We get all hung up on the means whereby a thing can be done.

Moses fell into this trap. The people had been eating manna, and they began to complain that they had no flesh to eat.

> The rabble with them began to crave other food, and again the Israelites started wailing and said, "If only we had meat to eat! We remember the fish we ate in Egypt at no cost — also the cucumbers, melons, leeks, onions and garlic. But now we have lost our appetite; we never see anything but this manna!" (Num. 11:4-6)

Moses began to complain to the Lord regarding the burden of the job. "He asked the Lord, 'Why have You brought this trouble on Your servant? What have I done to displease You that You put the burden of all these people on me? . . . I cannot carry all these people by myself; the burden is too heavy for me' " (vv. 11, 14).

The first thing the Lord did was provide some help for Moses.

> The Lord said to Moses, "Bring Me seventy of Israel's elders who are known to you as leaders and officials among the people. . . . I will take of the Spirit that is on you and put the Spirit on them. They will help you carry the burden of the people so that you will not have to carry it alone" (vv. 16-17).

Then the Lord promised that there would be flesh to eat—a change of diet. And it would be in abundance (see vv. 18-20).

Moses couldn't figure it out. How on earth could God find enough meat to feed all these people?

> But Moses said, "Here I am among six hundred thousand men on foot, and You say, 'I will give them meat to eat for a whole month!' Would they have enough if flocks and herds were slaughtered for them? Would they have enough if all the fish in the sea were caught for them?" (vv. 21-22)

He got involved in the means whereby this could be accomplished. Here was a God-given promise in plain Hebrew from the Creator of the universe, and Moses couldn't believe it. Why? Because he really didn't know God? No, he had spoken to God and knew His power. His problem was our problem. The details of the thing—the "means whereby"—the Lord would do it.

But God has His means.

> The Lord answered Moses, "Is the Lord's arm too short? You will now see whether or not what I say will come true for you." . . . Now a wind went out from the Lord and drove quail in from the sea. It brought them down all around the camp to about three feet above the ground, as far as a day's walk in any direction" (Num. 11:23, 31).

Another illustration of human doubt about God's supply is seen in the disciples' reaction to the Lord's concern for the physical welfare of the people who were following Him.

> During those days another large crowd gathered. Since they had nothing to eat, Jesus called His disciples to Him and said, "I have compassion for these people; they have already been with Me three days and have nothing to eat. . . ." His disciples answered, "But where in this remote place can anyone get enough bread to feed them?" (Mark 8:1-4)

But Jesus did it. He fed them with seven loaves and a few small fishes.

By contrast, consider the case of the women who had it on their hearts to anoint the body of their crucified Lord.

> Very early on the first day of the week, just after sunrise, they were on their way to the tomb and they asked each other, "Who will roll the stone away from the entrance of the tomb?" But when they looked up, they saw that the stone, which was very large, had been rolled away (16:2-4).

Their minds were not on the stone but on the objective. They had awakened with a desire to do something for the Lord, and they were undeterred by obstacles. The fact of the stone — or the guards at the tomb — didn't cause them to turn back. And the difficulties vanished before them when they pressed ahead in faith with their eyes on the goal. I imagine most of us would have gotten about halfway there, realized the futility of the idea, and returned to a warm bed for a few more hours of sleep.

Consider the twelve men sent by Moses to spy out the Promised Land. The report when they returned evidenced they were good intelligence agents. They had been diligent in their task. But it is interesting to note that their conclusions varied. Ten saw the difficulties — two saw the opportunities.

The report: "They gave Moses this account: 'We went into the land to which you sent us, and it does flow with milk and honey! Here is its fruit. But the people who live there are powerful, and the cities are fortified and very large' " (Num. 13:27-28).

The conclusion of the two: "We should go up and take possession of the land, for we can certainly do it" (v. 30).

The conclusion of the ten: "We can't attack those people; they are stronger than we are" (v. 31).

Admittedly, the people of the land were tough, and it was not going to be a Sunday School picnic. They were a fierce, immoral lot. The people of Canaan were not savages, but a highly developed race. But they were so vile and wicked that one historian says, "To destroy them was an act of mercy to the countries of the world. The happiness of the human race depended on it. If the Jews failed, the world would have been lost."

Caleb saw this as clearly as the rest, but note his words. He does not say, "Let us go up and take possession of the land, for we can certainly do it."

Caleb saw the thing from God's perspective. Of course, they were strong, but were they stronger than God? Was He not with Israel? Did He not go before them? Is anything too hard for Him? Of course, their cities are walled. But are they walled to heaven? Can God not peek over? Are they too high for Him?

The Bible makes it clear what their problem was. "Then they despised the pleasant land; they did not believe His promise. They grumbled in their tents and did not obey the Lord" (Ps. 106:24-25). *They didn't believe God.* They believed what they saw—and got their eyes off God. Of course, there were giants in the land, but when you think about it, there is only about fourteen inches difference between a giant and an average person. Think how both must look to God!

I have a friend named Bob Boardman who lives in Tokyo. Bob is a big, rugged ex-Marine, who stands well over six feet tall. When he walks down the streets of Tokyo, he looks huge. But if I were to go to the top of the Tokyo tower and look down at Bob and some of his friends, there wouldn't appear to be any difference. If that's true, think how they must look from God's viewpoint. So it all depends on one's perspective, one's point of view, the way one looks at things. Do we see things from a problem-centered perspective, or do we look at tasks with the promises of God in mind?

But here's an interesting thing to consider. The facts of the matter—the *real* facts were not at all as the spies supposed. They had supposed that the people looked upon them as grasshoppers. "We saw the Nephilim there (the descendants of Anak come from the Nephilim). We seemed like grasshoppers in our own eyes, and we looked the same to them" (Num. 13:33).

But how did the people really view them? One of them, the harlot Rahab said,

> I know that the Lord has given this land to you and that a great fear of you has fallen on us, so that all who live in this country are melting in fear because of you. We have heard how the Lord dried up the water of the Red Sea for you when you came out of Egypt, and what you did to Sihon and Og, the two kings of the Amorites east of the Jordan, whom you completely destroyed. When we heard of it, our hearts sank and everyone's courage failed because of you, for the Lord your God is God in heaven above and on the earth below (Josh. 2:9-11).

Isn't that something! The people of the land were living in terror, knowing they were doomed. They had heard of the Exodus from Egypt and the miracle at the Red Sea. Ever since, they had dreaded the day when they would have to face these people whose God fought for them so mightily and performed miracles and wonders in their behalf. Their hearts melted and there was no more courage left in any of them.

Yet the people of God fainted for fear. They said in effect that God was not able to fulfill His word. He had undertaken more than He could perform . . . bitten off more than He could chew.

They saw the obstacles, but were blind to God. There are those who think that the ability to see obstacles is a mark of maturity and insight. Really, this is the easiest thing to see. God wants people who see the way over the difficulty and give encouragement to the people.

What was the result of the report of the ten spies? "That night all the people of the community raised their voices and wept aloud" (Num. 14:1). Discouragement inevitably resulted from believing these men and looking at circumstances rather than believing God. But Caleb and Joshua said,

> The land we passed through and explored is exceedingly good. If the Lord is pleased with us, He will lead

us into that land, a land flowing with milk and honey, and will give it to us. Only do not rebel against the Lord. And do not be afraid of the people of the land, because we will swallow them up. Their protection is gone, but the Lord is with us. Do not be afraid of them (vv. 7-9).

Ultimately only Joshua and Caleb entered the Promised Land. The complainers, the doubters, the negative thinkers bleached their bones in the wilderness.

We must keep our eyes on our objectives not on the obstacles!

So, to review, when you undertake a task for God, remember three things:

1. Get right at it.
2. Trust God for the help you need.
3. Focus on objectives, not obstacles.

Of course, obstacles and difficulties can be very real and very serious. We can't expect them simply to go away just because we think positively. In the next chapter we will discuss how to resolve difficulties.

Chapter Nine

Resolving Difficulties

The skies are not always blue. Storms are as much a part of life as starlight. This fact can sometimes throw leaders into a quandary. They are serving the Lord, doing the will of God from the heart, but in the midst of it all they find themselves facing difficulties, dilemmas, and problems.

Difficulties for leaders usually come in two forms: problems with the group and problems in their own personal lives.

The Example of Moses

The Scriptures are filled with examples of people of God who ran into difficulties as they held positions of leadership. Moses was one. He ran into a problem at one point in his life because he tried to do everything himself. Some people are like that. Their philosophy is "If you want a job done right, you've got to do it yourself."

An admirable feature about Moses in his situation was that he was personally involved with the people. He was not a non-working supervisor. But his strength became his weakness. "The next day Moses took his seat to serve as judge for the people, and they stood around him from morning till evening" (Ex. 18:13). He was giving himself all day to a group of people who had recently tried to stone him to death. To serve and help people who appreciate what you are doing is relatively easy, but Moses was giving his time and energy to a crowd of ungrateful people, who were hateful, unappreciative, and thoughtless, and who had tried to take his life. Moses was a servant of God and was demonstrating a Godlike spirit before them.

One day Moses' father-in-law saw what he was doing and asked him about it. "When his father-in-law saw all that Moses was doing for the people, he said, 'What is this you are doing for the people? Why do you alone sit as judge, while all these people stand around you from morning till evening?' " (v. 14)

Moses replied, "Because the people come to me to seek God's will. Whenever they have a dispute, it is brought to me, and I decide between the parties and inform them of God's decrees and laws" (vv. 15-16).

When Jethro heard this explanation, he gave Moses some sound advice:

> What you are doing is not good. You and these people who come to you will only wear yourselves out. The work is too heavy for you; you cannot handle it alone. Listen now to me and I will give you some advice, and may God be with you. You must be the people's representative before God and bring their disputes to Him. Teach them the decrees and laws, and show them the way to live and the duties they are to perform. But select capable men from all the people—men who fear God, trustworthy men who hate dishonest gain—and appoint them as officials over thousands, hundreds, fifties and tens. Have them serve as judges for the people at all times, but have them bring every difficult case to you; the simple cases they can decide themselves. That will make your load lighter, because they will share it with you. If you do this and God so commands, you will be able to stand the strain, and all these people will go home satisfied (vv. 17-23).

One of the most amazing things in this record was the fact that Moses had the good sense to take that advice. Pride could have kept him from it. He could have said, "Who do you think you are, telling *me* what to do? Don't you know who I am? I am Moses, the man who has spoken to God Himself face to face. If I want advice I'll go right to the top and get it—I'll go to God Himself. I don't need one of my in-laws to come along and tell me what to do!" How easy it would have been for Moses to react like that! But he didn't! "Moses listened to his father-in-law and did everything he said" (v. 24).

Now let's look more closely at the advice that got Moses out of his difficulties. Four things stand out.

1. Moses' number one priority as a leader was to pray for the people under his charge. "You must be the people's representative before God and bring their disputes to Him." You therefore as a leader must make this your number one task. If you're a Sunday School teacher, pray for each member of your class by name. If you are the head of a department in the church, pray for those who report to you. If you are a pastor, elder, or deacon, pray for those who are under your care. "Epaphras, who is one of you and a servant of Christ Jesus, sends greetings. He is always wrestling in prayer for you, that you may stand firm in all the will of God, mature and fully assured" (Col. 4:12). Praying for people will do a great deal to resolve problems or nip them in the bud.

2. Moses was to teach the Word of God. "Teach them the decrees and laws." Whether publicly or privately, whether to the entire congregation or to one individual, the leader must help people learn what the Bible says and help them apply its truths to their everyday situations. People can't *do* the truth if they don't *know* the truth. Jesus prayed, "Sanctify them by the truth; Your word is truth" (John 17:17).

3. Moses was to be a visible example to his people. He had to "show them the *way to live,* and the *duties they are to perform.*" It has been well said, "Tell them what, tell them why, and show them how."

Dawson Trotman, the founder of The Navigators, used to say to us, "Telling is not teaching; listening is not learning."

The leader must show the people by example how to walk with God and how to work for God. People need help in learning how to live for Christ and how to serve Him. And people don't learn that from lectures and sermons. They must be shown. Like a dressmaker, they need a pattern to follow, and the best pattern is the example that is set by the leader.

4. Moses was to delegate his responsibilities. Jethro finally got to the main issue. He told Moses to share the load with other men. "Have them serve as judges for the people at all times, but have them bring every difficult case to you; the simple cases they can decide themselves. That will make your load lighter, because they will share it with you" (Ex. 18:22). Moses must stop trying to do it all himself. He must share the load. But he must choose his associates carefully. They must have spiritual depth, be properly related to God, to others, and to the world around them—"able men, such as fear God, men of truth, hating covetousness."

Getting the right person in the job is a blessing; getting the wrong person can be a curse. Remember that it is easier to get people into a position than to get them out. Careful selection of coworkers is a hallmark of a good leader. In the advice Jethro gave Moses, he taught him something of his personal priorities, the basics of his job, and the art of delegation. Any job, no matter how large and complex it is, can be broken down into workable and manageable units if we have the right people to place in charge.

Leaders-in-training

Those to whom responsibilities are delegated are actually leaders-in-training. They are colaborers. Three qualities must characterize the people you put in charge.

1. Likemindedness is a prerequisite to colaborship in the job. "I have no one else like him, who takes a genuine interest in your welfare. For everyone looks out for their own interests, not those of Jesus Christ" (Phil. 2:20-21). Your coworkers must agree with your goals and objectives. In fact, they must be their own. You in turn should be eager to allow them to carry them out in their own way, using their own methods and plans that are in line with the gifts and abilities that God has given them. The idea is this: agreement on goals; much latitude on methods and means.

Ezra and Nehemiah exemplify this principle. Each led a group of people from Babylon to Jerusalem. When Ezra started out, God gave him an idea as to how to proceed with his plan.

> There, by the Ahava Canal, I proclaimed a fast, so that we might humble ourselves before our God and ask Him for a safe journey for us and our children, with all our possessions. I was ashamed to ask the king for soldiers and horsemen to protect us from enemies on the road, because we had told the king, "The good hand of our God is on everyone who looks to Him, but His great anger is against all who forsake Him." So we fasted and petitioned our God about this, and He answered our prayer (Ezra 8:21-23).

He was convinced that to go to the king and ask for help would be a sin. He would fast and pray and launch out, trusting in God alone to take him and his people safely to Jerusalem.

Some years later Nehemiah felt led of God to undertake a similar project. His objective was the same: to take a group of people from Babylon to Jerusalem. But look at *his* approach!

> I also said to him, "If it pleases the king, may I have letters to the governors of Trans-Euphrates, so that they will provide me safe-conduct until I arrive in Judah? And may I have a letter to Asaph, keeper of the king's forest, so he will give me timber to make beams for the gates of the citadel by the temple and for the city wall and for the residence I will occupy?" And because the gracious hand of my God was upon me, the king granted my requests. So I went to the governors of Trans-Euphrates and gave them the king's let-

ters. The king had also sent army officers and cavalry
with me (Neh. 2:7-9).

Ezra had felt it would be wrong for him to ask for human
help. But not Nehemiah! He didn't want to set foot outside the
city without letters to the governors and captains of the army
and horse soldiers. He wanted all the help he could get. Now,
who was right! The answer is simple: They were *both* right.
God led one man to do it one way and the other to do it
another way. But here is where we often get hung up. My
method is this way and yours is that? Therefore you must be
wrong! Not so. The objective must be clear, well defined, and
fixed. But methods may vary.

Notice how Ezra handled the problem of sin in the camp:
"When I heard this, I tore my tunic and cloak, pulled hair from
my head and beard and sat down appalled" (Ezra 9:3).

When Nehemiah found sin in the camp, he dealt with it in an
entirely different way.

> But I warned them and said, "Why do you spend the
> night by the wall? If you do this again, I will lay hands
> on you." From that time on they no longer came on
> the Sabbath. . . . I rebuked them and called curses
> down on them. I beat some of the men and pulled out
> their hair. I made them take an oath in God's name and
> said: "You are not to give your daughters in marriage
> to their sons, nor are you to take their daughters in
> marriage for your sons or for yourselves" (Neh. 13:21,
> 25).

Again, they handled the problem differently. Ezra sat down
and pulled out his hair. When Nehemiah discovered the people
living in sin, he pulled out theirs! Who was right? They were
both right. The objective was to get rid of sin among the people. The methods of accomplishing the objective were completely different. So when you give people jobs, allow them the
flexibility to exercise their God-given abilities as long as their
approach is Christ-honoring and scriptural. But likemindedness
is essential with regard to objectives.

2. *Maturity* is another prerequisite. Your colaborer must "not be a recent convert, or he may become conceited and fall under the same judgment as the devil" (1 Tim. 3:6). They must be able to handle the emotional impact of carrying responsibility. Two things happen to people when they are given a load to carry in the program of the church. The responsibility makes them or breaks them.

I have watched young men and women grow and blossom, and I have seen them crash. Those who grew were those who accepted responsibility with a humble spirit and depended on the Lord for His sustaining grace and power. God used the added responsibility to cause them to exercise greater dependence on Him. It drove them to their knees and got them searching the Scriptures for guidance. They became stronger people, eventually able to carry a greater load.

On the other hand, I've watched people get a job and seen them set back in their walk with God. They became overbearing and dictatorial. Pride welled up in their lives and they suffered the consequences. God resisted them, and they went nowhere.

It is important, therefore, for leaders to know their people and lead them step by step along the road of responsibility. "Do not be hasty in the laying on of hands, and do not share in the sins of others. Keep yourself pure" (1 Tim. 5:22). One of the best ways of doing this is to give people a little responsibility and see how it affects them. If they can handle it, they are ready for more. Leaders who know how to delegate and share the load with others are a blessing to their people. They will grow and develop and become spiritually qualified workers in a world where the laborers are few.

3. *Faithfulness* is the third necessary quality in a coworker. The Bible says, "A faithful man who can find?" (Prov. 20:6) Admittedly, this person is a rare bird. It is difficult to find people you can count on fully. It seems that dependability is not one of the characteristics of our age. Maybe it never has been. "Help, Lord, for the godly are no more; the faithful have vanished from among men" (Ps. 12:1).

Nevertheless, leaders will do well to wait for the faithful person to come along before they begin to share the load. Solomon gives us the reason: "Like a bad tooth or a lame foot is reliance on the unfaithful in times of trouble" (Prov. 25:19).

Two Scriptures I share with people in trying to help build faithfulness into their lives express principles that Jesus taught His disciples. The first is the importance of *faithfulness in little things.* "Whoever can be trusted with very little can also be trusted with much, and whoever is dishonest with very little will also be dishonest with much" (Luke 16:10). The person who cannot see the importance of doing a small job faithfully will be the same person who fails in the larger tasks. You can tell much about people by watching how they set up chairs for a meeting or greet people as they arrive. It is quite easy to detect whether or not their hearts are in it. People who do a sloppy job in lining up the transportation for the class weekend retreat will do the same kind of job when they are asked to run the retreat.

The second principle is *faithfulness in working with others.* "And if you have not been trustworthy with someone else's property, who will give you property of your own?" (Luke 16:12) Some people just hate to be called on to help another person in their program. If it's not totally their own deal, they would just as soon not do it. Jesus taught that before you can have a responsibility that is your own, you must learn to work with others and help them with their responsibilities.

That's why there is always room at the top. So few people are willing to learn how to handle ultimate responsibility by first fitting into the life and schedule and program of another. But the Scriptures are loaded with examples of this very thing. Joshua was "Moses' minister." Elisha was chosen as the one who "went after Elijah and ministered unto him." Each of these men became a great leader in his own right, but they first learned that demonstrating these basic characteristics is blessed indeed. Leaders will be able to delegate a good share of their workload to others and rejoice as the work goes forward in accomplishing the mission of the church.

Keeping Others Informed

The second area where leaders can hit some pretty rough snags is in assuming that people know what is going on or in thinking everybody knows why leaders do things as they do. Moses ran into this problem: "Moses thought that his own people would realize that God was using him to rescue them, but they did not" (Acts 7:25). Leaders soon learn to keep the lines of communication open. If they don't, it can lead to disaster.

This is vividly illustrated in the history of the Children of Israel. The wars of conquest had been forgotten, and the land enjoyed peace. "So the Lord gave Israel all the land He had sworn to give their forefathers, and they took possession of it and settled there" (Josh. 21:43). The tribes that had their farms on the other side of the Jordan returned to their homes. En route they built an altar by the Jordan River (22:10). Then a strange and terrible thing happened. Hearing of the altar and imagining the worst, the rest of the Children of Israel made plans to go to war against their brethren for idolatry!

Scripture describes the situation as follows: "And when the Israelites heard that they had built the altar on the border of Canaan at Geliloth near the Jordan on the Israelite side, the whole assembly of Israel gathered at Shiloh to go to war against them" (vv. 11-12). Imagine that!

After years of war — after years of being comrades-in-arms — they made plans for a civil war. Why? It was a simple misunderstanding that arose because the lines of communication were not open. The majority had only "heard" indirectly of the actions of the minority and knew nothing of the reasons behind their actions.

Happily, the majority sent a delegation across the river to determine the facts. The explanation was simple. The altar was

"not for burnt offerings or sacrifices." On the contrary, it is to be a witness between us and you and the generations that follow, that we will worship the Lord at his sanctuary with our burnt offerings, sacrifices and fellowship offerings. Then in the future your descendants will not be able to say to ours, "You have no share in the Lord" (vv. 26-27).

When the delegation heard the explanation, they were satisfied, and the matter was dropped (22:30). Disaster was avoided. But note the pattern: hasty suspicion led to false accusations, which led to anger and division, which could have led to war. Leaders must do what they can to prevent such situations by keeping people informed. Plans laid in secret have a way of bringing forth a negative response. An active endeavor to help people see what is being done and why it is being done will go a long way on stopping the rumor mill.

Most leaders agree that good communication is needed and at the same time is tremendously difficult. The problem is compounded by the fact that in many cases the real source of dissension and division is the devil. One of his chief tools in disrupting the program of the church and stopping the thrust of the Gospel is to get Christians fighting among themselves. Leaders must do everything they can to maintain a climate of love, peace, and harmony among their people. And that takes effort. "Be completely humble and gentle; be patient, bearing with one another in love. Make every effort to keep the unity of the Spirit through the bond of peace" (Eph. 4:2-3).

A personal report to the people or an occasional newsletter helps. Asking people's advice and letting them in on decisions is very helpful in many ways. For one thing, leaders usually need all the help they can get. Second, the people know they are in on the action and are making real contributions. This keeps morale high and misunderstandings to a minimum. This is a task leaders can't duck. They must face the responsibility of keeping information flowing and the lines of communication open. Though it's hard work and sometimes a pain in the neck, they'll be glad they did.

Doing Unpleasant Tasks

When leaders major on those things that they enjoy doing and shirk tasks that are unpleasant to them, problems arise. There are many responsibilities involved in the leaders' job, and they must be willing to fulfill them all. David is a classic example of this. David was a man who excelled in battle. He was a warrior, and a good one. He also ran the affairs of the people ably. He did not neglect the administrative duties of his office just because he preferred the excitement of leadership in battle.

> David reigned over all Israel, doing what was just and right for all his people. Joab son of Zeruiah was over the army; Jehoshaphat son of Ahilud was recorder; Zadok son of Ahitub and Ahimelech son of Abiathar were priests; Shavsha was secretary; Benaiah son of Jehoiada was over the Kerethites and Pelethites; and David's sons were chief officials at the king's side (1 Chron. 18:14-17).

David had two supreme military officers, one to command forces in the field and the other, David's bodyguard, to keep order at home. He had two religious officers under Abiathar. He also had two civil officers, one to keep him abreast of the business that needed to be done and the other to keep the public informed of what had been done. The people thus were made aware of any new laws and kept in personal touch with the king. It worked well. The people loved him.

It is the leaders' job to keep a well-balanced program underway. It is so easy for them to promote one aspect of the job at the expense of another. They can get a fund drive going and neglect evangelism. They can have a strong evangelistic thrust and neglect the training of their people. They can be so concerned about the organizational aspect and administrative details that they lose sight of the broad objectives. Imbalance usually comes when leaders allow themselves to focus on work that they enjoy while avoiding the attendant responsibilities that are a part of the job. The ability to take the bitter with the sweet is one of the marks of a good leader.

Personal Problems: Sorrow and Affliction

Leaders are not exempt from the personal problems of life. Financial difficulties may plague them. They may face severe testings with their children. Sickness in the family may bring a burden tough to cope with. They may face personal attacks on their motives or character or integrity. The storms of life may rage around them and appear at times to overwhelm them in their fury. Heartache, concern, and perplexity are not strangers to the person in a position of leadership.

The Apostle Paul talked about this:

> Not only so, but we also rejoice in our sufferings, because we know that suffering produces perseverance; perseverance, character; and character, hope. And hope does not disappoint us, because God has poured out His love into our hearts by the Holy Spirit, whom He has given us (Rom. 5:3-5).

When I read that passage, I am struck with the fact that the apostle says we glory or rejoice in tribulation. Why? What's so neat about tribulation? Why would a perfectly normal, sane person glory in it? To most of us, tribulation is to be avoided, but here it is presented as something to be gloried in. This is a strange paradox for tribulation surely means pressure, affliction, and trouble.

The word rendered *tribulation* here comes from a term for an ancient threshing instrument by which wheat was separated from chaff. This gives us a clue as to why Paul gloried in it. And not only Paul. Other New Testament writers bring out the same idea. Peter wrote, "Do not be surprised at the painful trial you are suffering, as though something strange were happening to you" (1 Peter 4:12). James tells us, "Consider it pure joy, my brothers, whenever you face trials of many kinds, because you know that the testing of your faith develops perseverance. Perseverance must finish its work so that you may be mature and complete, not lacking anything" (James 1:2-4).

Amazing! My natural tendency is to count it all joy when I climb *out of* divers temptations, not when I fall into them!

The Apostle Paul told the Colossians to respond to extended suffering with joyfulness and thanksgiving! "Being strengthened with all power according to His glorious might so that you may have great endurance and patience, and joyfully giving thanks to the Father, who has qualified you to share in the inheritance of the saints in the kingdom of light" (Col. 1:11-12).

As we read these passages, we can see why trials and troubles are to be welcomed with thanksgiving and joy. It is through them that God builds Christian character. Endurance and staying power are produced in our lives. We must not lose sight of God's way of doing things. Endurance is a basic quality essential to leadership, and this is God's method of making it a part of us. A tree raised in a hothouse is perfectly healthy but is tall and spindly. A tree that grows where the wind blows hard sinks its roots down deep. It is rugged, strong, and has staying power. That's what leaders need. When trials come, they strengthen our faith, and the experience produces confidence in God for the future.

Paul writes,

> But He said to me, "My grace is sufficient for you, for My power is made perfect in weakness." Therefore I will boast all the more gladly about my weaknesses, so that Christ's power may rest on me. That is why, for Christ's sake, I delight in weaknesses, in insults, in hardships, in persecutions, in difficulties. For when I am weak, then I am strong (2 Cor. 12:9-10).

We must face the fact that God is more concerned with our completeness (maturity) than our comfort. It is His desire that the many facets of the beauty of Christ may shine through our lives.

Have you ever visited a pottery factory. When the pottery is placed in the kiln, its colors are dull and muted. After it has been in the fire—when it comes out of the oven—its colors are vivid. The fire makes it beautiful. So it is in our lives. The fires of life bring out the beauty of the life of Christ within.

Lila Trotman, the wife of the founder of The Navigators, has faced many a storm. But when Lila walks into a room, the place lights up. She radiates a beauty and freshness of spirit that is a wonder to behold. The beauty of Christ shines through her.

This only happens, of course, when we face the tribulations of life in the light of the cross of Christ. Otherwise adversity can drive a wedge between us and the Lord. We may become bitter. So we must face up to our troubles and trust God to use them to accomplish His purposes and to do His work in us.

In addition to manifesting the beauty of Christ, tribulations can be used to demonstrate the power of God. Paul and Silas had been beaten, thrown into prison, and put into the stocks. In spite of the fact that their civil rights had been violated and they were treated unlawfully, what do we find them doing? Singing! Protest songs? No! They were singing songs of praise to God.

Paul practiced in Philippi what he preached in his letter to the Colossians. When they suffered long, they were to respond with thanksgiving and joy. This would be a manifestation of the almighty, glorious power of God at work in them. "Being strengthened with all power according to His glorious might so that you may have great endurance and patience, and joyfully giving thanks to the Father" (Col. 1:11-12).

There is a great deal of discussion concerning how the power of God is manifested in a life. Paul tells us that when a person is going through the flames of adversity with the spirit of joy and thanksgiving, that's power.

And as Moses turned aside to observe the bush that burned but was not consumed, so people are challenged by the life that comes through the fires singing the praises of God.

One of the most helpful Scriptures to keep in mind during difficult days is given to us by Isaiah: " 'For My thoughts are not your thoughts, neither are your ways My ways,' declares the Lord. 'As the heavens are higher than the earth, so are My ways higher than your ways and My thoughts than your thoughts' " (Isa. 55:8-9). As we pray for deliverance, we must keep in mind that God has His own timetable and ways. This is illustrated clearly in the experience of the Apostle Paul. At Antioch of Pisidia he was thrown out of town (Acts 13:50). He went from there to Iconium, where they tried to stone him, but he escaped (14:5-6). He fled next to Lystra, where he was stoned and left for dead (v. 19). That's two escapes out of three possible assaults, which isn't bad according to the law of averages, though a person can hardly afford even one miss of this magnitude, since it's likely to be fatal!

In recounting this tale, Paul, however, makes an astounding statement:

> You, however, know all about my teaching, my way of life, my purpose, faith, patience, love, endurance, persecutions, sufferings — what kinds of things happened to me in Antioch, Iconium and Lystra, the persecutions I endured. Yet the Lord rescued me from all of them (2 Tim. 3:10-11).

Did Paul really mean "from all of them"? At Antioch, yes; at Iconium, yes; but at Lystra he was stoned and left for dead.

Still Paul says he was delivered out of them all, and herein lies a beautiful truth. Paul was delivered twice *from* the stones and once *through* them! But in each case it was the deliverance of God. Paul would, no doubt, have chosen to be delivered from them in *each* case, but God's ways are not always ours. Paul came through these experiences with a glowing testimony to the delivering and preserving power of God. "The Lord will rescue me from every evil attack and will bring me safely to His heavenly kingdom. To Him be glory for ever and ever. Amen" (4:18).

"And we know that in all things God works for the good of those who love Him, who have been called according to His purpose" (Rom. 8:28). The truth of this statement is easy to understand, but it's hard to live out in daily life. When the leader is in the midst of the furnace of affliction, it is tough to have that assurance.

While I am writing this, my wife is making an apple pie. If she were to offer me a handful of vegetable shortening to eat for lunch, I'd say, "No thanks." The same would be true if she offered me a cup of flour or some baking powder, flour, and shortening. But when she puts these ingredients in the mixing bowl with others, works them all together, and places the mixture in the heat of the oven for a while, then it is a different story.

That's what God often does with our lives. He works together a blend of good times and tough times, and He knows the exact mixture that is good for us. We go through the fires of tribulation, and when the process is complete, we are better people for it. The secret is to realize what God is doing and "glory in tribulations"; to respond with thanksgiving and joy.

So when you find yourself troubled or perplexed or persecuted or cast down, rejoice! God is building endurance and hope. "Perseverance must finish its work so that you may be mature and complete, not lacking anything" (James 1:4). And if you are facing these things now, cheer up! You're in mighty good company. Paul wrote, "We are hard pressed on every side, but not crushed; perplexed, but not in despair; persecuted, but not abandoned; struck down, but not destroyed" (2 Cor. 4:8-9). In addition to that, Paul was constantly facing death. "For we who are alive are always being given over to death for Jesus' sake, so that His life may be revealed in our mortal body" (v. 11).

What kept Paul going in the face of all this? He lists five things. The first was faith. "It is written: 'I believed; therefore I have spoken.' With that same spirit of faith we also believe and therefore speak" (v. 13). The second was hope. "Because we know that the one who raised the Lord Jesus from the dead will also raise us with Jesus and present us with you in His presence" (v. 14). The third was the needs of others. "If we are out of our mind, it is for the sake of God; if we are in our right mind, it is for you" (5:13). The fourth was the benefit of his own soul. "Therefore we do not lose heart. Though outwardly we are wasting away, yet inwardly we are being renewed day by day" (4:16). The fifth was the fact that he viewed everything in the light of eternity. "For our light and momentary troubles are achieving for us an eternal glory that far outweighs them all. So we fix our eyes not on what is seen, but on what is unseen. For what is seen is temporary, but what is unseen is eternal" (vv. 17-18).

If we can keep things in perspective, present suffering, which seems heavy and long, is really light and short. But we must face adversity in the light of the cross and the perspective of heaven and remember it is working for our good—not against us.

What are some practical steps leaders can take when they are in the midst of trouble and sorrow? First of all they can take Scripture seriously. "Cast all your anxiety on Him because He cares for you" (1 Peter 5:7).

I had memorized this verse as a new Christian, but it wasn't until sometime later that the full truth of it became part of my experience. I was talking with Dr. Bill Bright of Campus Crusade for Christ, sharing with him some of the heartaches and difficulties I was experiencing.

He looked at me and said, "LeRoy, I have found great comfort in 1 Peter 5:7." He went on, "I have concluded in my own life that either I carry my burdens or Jesus does. We cannot both carry them, and I've decided to cast them on Him."

He challenged me to try it. I left that motel room bewildered. Did that verse actually mean what it said? I went to my room and began to pray. To the best of my ability I did what Bill had said. For months I had carried a heavy knot in my stomach. I could actually feel the thing leaving. I experienced the deliverance of God. No, the problem did not go away, and hasn't to this day. But the burden is gone. I no longer spend sleepless nights or cry myself to sleep. I can honestly face the burdens with a joyful spirit and thankfulness of heart.

During their journeys, the Children of Israel, "When they came to Marah, they could not drink its water because it was bitter" (Ex. 15:23). This was followed by Elim, where they found sweet water and fruitful palms. "Then they came to Elim, where there were twelve springs and seventy palm trees, and they camped there near the water" (v. 27).

I know that in my own life, the bitter waters of Marah have been followed by sweeter fellowship with my Lord and greater fruitfulness in His service.

Chapter Ten

Surviving Dangers

Rattlesnakes are fairly common where I live. I encounter one almost every summer. It is a frightening experience to see a rattlesnake coiled, looking at you, ready to strike. It's lightning quick and accurate. I have a two-point program for rattlesnakes; shun and avoid. You don't need much insight to figure out what to do with something as dangerous as an old diamondback rattler. You don't mess around.

A friend of mine tried to pick up a rattlesnake once. He ended up in the hospital. It didn't kill him — got him with one fang only — but Bob was a mighty sick young man. His finger, where it bit him, is all shriveled up today. One advantage in dealing with these snakes is they don't try to trick you. When they shake their rattles and show you their fangs, you know what you are up against.

Unfortunately that's not so with many of the dangers that can kill off a leader. All too often these menaces appear to be harmless or masquerade behind a cloak of respectability. Some, on the other hand, come right out in the open and leave you with no doubt in your mind. They show their fangs. You know where you stand. Let's look at some dangers to leadership.

Some years ago I was gathering some men around me to make a thrust for Christ among university students. Bob Stephens, a young Air Force officer who was separated from the service, wrote a letter to me expressing an interest in the program. I wrote back and told him I had a couple of questions I wanted to ask.

The first was "Do you think we can involve fellows in this ministry who hate God?" Bob is a brilliant young man, an honors graduate from the School of Engineering at the University of Maryland. It didn't take him long to figure out the answer. When he replied no, I sent him this Scripture: "No one can serve two masters. Either he will hate the one and love the other, or he will be devoted to the one and despise the other. You cannot serve both God and Money" (Matt. 6:24).

With the verse I sent another question: "Do you think we can have men working with us who are enemies of the cross of Christ?" He said no. So I sent him another verse:

Join with others in following my example, brothers, and take note of those who live according to the pattern we gave you. For, as I have often told you before and now say again even with tears, many live as enemies of the cross of Christ. Their destiny is destruction, their god is their stomach, and their glory is in their shame. Their mind is on earthly things (Phil. 3:17-19).

In that passage Paul says that the enemies of the cross "mind earthly things." They are all wrapped up in the things of this world and as such are living exactly opposite to the spirit of the cross, which is one of self-sacrificing love.

Bob agreed. He came with a desire to give of himself. For many years he has served in that spirit. The sin of covetousness has never gripped his soul. God has used him greatly around the world. Young people on three continents trace their spiritual roots to the influence of Christ through Bob's life.

Covetousness

Covetousness is one of those sins totally repudiated by the Apostle Paul. "You know we never used flattery, nor did we put on a mask to cover up greed—God is our witness" (1 Thes. 2:5). Personal gain was not a motive that lurked in the shadows of his ministry. If it had, he would not have been used as he was in the ministry of planting thriving churches.

Furthermore, Paul would not have been practicing what he preached. He told the Colossians,

> Since, then, you have been raised with Christ, set your hearts on things above, where Christ is seated at the right hand of God. Set your minds on things above, not on earthly things. . . . Put to death, therefore, whatever belongs to your earthly nature: sexual immorality, impurity, lust, evil desires and greed, which is idolatry (Col. 3:1-2, 5).

Note that covetousness is idolatry, and the Apostle John also writes, "Dear children, keep yourselves from idols" (1 John 5:21).

Why is covetousness so deadly to spiritual leaders? For at least two reasons. One, covetousness makes leaders lose their perspective—their lives become focused on *this* world. Jesus said, "My kingdom is not of this world" (John 18:36). If the leaders are occupied with the things of this world, their minds are diverted into unprofitable pursuits. They are living for the temporal rather than the eternal.

Jesus lived and died to bring *eternal* life to the world. The leaders therefore must not live to enhance their own circumstances with personal gain. Because of the subtlety of this danger, they must constantly be on guard, heeding John's warning:

> Do not love the world or anything in the world. If anyone loves the world, the love of the Father is not in him. For everything in the world—the cravings of sinful man, the lust of his eyes and the boasting of what he has and does—comes not from the Father but from the world. The world and its desires pass away, but the man who does the will of God lives forever (1 John 2:15-17).

I once heard an evangelist brag that he could preach for two weeks and never wear the same suit twice! The scandal of people who heap up treasure to themselves has been a blot on the ministry.

This is not to say that the work of Christ should not be well-financed. The New Testament notes that the apostles had ample funds. It was common for people to sell their possessions and goods for the advancement of the work. Barnabas "sold a field he owned and brought the money and put it at the apostles' feet" (Acts 4:37). But the money did not go to enhance the apostles' personal fortunes. Peter said, "I have no silver or gold" (3:6).

The second reason covetousness is so deadly is that when a person gives God second place, soon He has no place at all. Covetousness is an insidious sin that grows in the hidden places of the heart. God said, "You shall have no other gods before Me" (Ex. 20:3). Idolatry is loving anything more than God. Today few gods are made of stone or tree stumps. Most of the gods of this world are composed of tinted glass, baked-on enamel, and chrome, or dacron and wool, or silk, or alligator leather.

I recall an incident with a young man who aspired to leadership in the cause of Christ. He and I were having a discussion at the Bible school from which he was to graduate that spring. He had done well academically and seemed to have great potential for God. I asked him what he was going to do upon graduation. He grew reflective, and I could see that he was thinking deeply. I began to wonder what he was going to say. Did he aspire to be a missionary in some remote jungle? Would he risk his life to take the Gospel behind the iron curtain? My imagination ran wild.

Finally he looked up at me and in earnest and serious tones said, "I think I'll buy a Buick!"

My heart sank. I was dumbfounded! Here was a man with potential for God's service whose mind was taken up with the passing glitter of this life. The command of Paul had not sunk in enough to govern his inner motivation: "Do not conform any longer to the pattern of this world, but be transformed by the renewing of your mind. Then you will be able to test and approve what God's will is—His good, pleasing and perfect will" (Rom. 12:2). The love of Christ was not pressing in on him to impel him to higher and nobler goals (see 2 Cor. 5:14-15).

The issue, of course, is not whether we are rich or poor. Some of the wealthiest people I know are dedicated men and women of God, who occupy strategic places of leadership in the cause of Christ. Covetousness is a condition of the heart, not the pocketbook. The things of this life can be used for Christ. Possessions can be as slaves or masters. They can hold us or we can use them. The person who has wealth and uses it wisely can be a blessing to hundreds of people.

People who are caught in the grip of covetousness are pitiful to behold. Satisfaction eludes them—all the way to the grave. "Whoever loves money never has money enough; whoever loves wealth is never satisfied with his income. This too is meaningless" (Ecc. 5:10).

Paul warns two classes of people. The first are those who live *to get rich.*

People who want to get rich fall into temptation and a trap and into many foolish and harmful desires that plunge men into ruin and destruction. For the love of money is a root of all kinds of evil. Some people, eager for money, have wandered from the faith and pierced themselves with many griefs (1 Tim. 6:9-10).

Such a snare is a very real threat. It struck close to Paul himself when Demas forsook Paul: "For Demas, because he loved this world, has deserted me and has gone to Thessalonica" (2 Tim. 4:10). Though he was a companion of the great apostle, Demas failed to heed this warning. It was his undoing.

The second group warned *are those who are rich.*

Command those who are rich in this present world not to be arrogant nor to put their hope in wealth, which is so uncertain, but to put their hope in God, who richly provides us with everything for our enjoyment. Command them to do good, to be rich in good deeds, and to be generous and willing to share. In this way they will lay up treasure for themselves as a firm foundation for the coming age, so that they may take hold of the life that is truly life (1 Tim. 6:17-19).

The rich are tempted to pride, to trust in the wealth of this world and not in God. They must live with eternity in mind, and use their wealth accordingly.

Jesus spoke on this topic as well. A man, thinking himself wronged by his brother, came to Jesus and said,

"Teacher, tell my brother to divide the inheritance with me." Jesus replied, "Man, who appointed Me a judge or an arbiter between you?" Then He said to them, "Watch out! Be on your guard against all kinds of greed; a man's life does not consist in the abundance of his possessions" (Luke 12:13-15).

Jesus did not sympathize with the man who claimed he was being cheated by his brother. He tried to raise everyone there from the sin of covetousness. One man had the money and the other wanted it. They were both in the clutches of covetousness. Jesus then told a parable that describes as a fool the man who "stores up things for himself but is not rich toward God" (v. 21).

Leaders will do well to search their hearts on this matter to make certain they are not sliding into this subtle and deadly trap.

Self-glory

The second deadly danger to leaders is pride. Paul wrote, "We were not looking for praise from men, not from you or anyone else" (1 Thes. 2:6). He had just repudiated the sin of covetousness (v. 5). Now he does the same with self-glory, the seeking of honor and prestige.

Here is another subtle trap. It happens so naturally that often one does not realize it. If you are a speaker at a conference or leading a group, things can take place to make you stand out as a very special person. It's happened to me: "There goes LeRoy Eims. He's leading one of the workshops at the conference." / "LeRoy, come over and chat for a minute. I have some friends who have been wanting to meet you." / "LeRoy, join us on the platform tonight, greet the congregation, and lead us in prayer." / "LeRoy, come join us at a special luncheon today. It's much quieter and more comfortable than eating in the dining room with the regular conferees."

Recently I was at a conference where some of these things were happening. I was falling into the trap of enjoying it and feeling important. I was having a quiet time on the second day, and the Holy Spirit spoke to me very directly and personally from the Word of God. I was reading in Mark and these verses stood out like a neon light:

> As He taught, Jesus said, "Watch out for the teachers of the law. They like to walk around in flowing robes and be greeted in the marketplaces, and have the most important seats in the synagogues and the places of honor at banquets. They devour widows' houses and for a show make lengthy prayers. Such men will be punished most severely" (Mark 12:38-40).

The Lord said in effect, "Do you love all these things that are happening, that make you feel important?"

"Yes, Lord."

"Do you love the salutation of people who feed your ego?"

"Yes, Lord."

"Do you love going up on the platform and being seen with all those important people?"

"Yes, Lord."

I reread the passage a number of times, then went to my knees, confessed my sins, and got right with the Lord. I sensed His comfort and forgiveness. Thank God for His promise: "If we confess our sins, He is faithful and just and will forgive us our sins and purify us from all unrighteousness" (1 John 1:9).

God's forgiveness was so complete that I found I could kid

myself about the whole thing. It all seemed so empty and stupid once the Holy Spirit had brought it into the open. When I would enter the hall on the ensuing days of the conference, I would admonish myself, "OK, dummy, don't act like a teacher of the Law." I'm sure many people who saw me wondered what I was smiling about. But I knew. I was amused by the foolishness and stupidity of seeking glory and was enjoying a renewed sense of closeness to God.

The leader will do well not to underestimate the danger of which the Apostle Paul warned when he wrote, "Let us not be desirous of vainglory." An incident in Paul's life illustrates his personal fear of human worship. Barnabas and Paul were being mightily used of God at Lystra, so much so that the people said, "The gods have come down to us in human form!" (Acts 14:11) When the apostles realized that the people intended to offer sacrifices to them as gods, "they tore their clothes and rushed into the crowd, shouting: 'Men, why are you doing this? We too are only men, human like you. We are bringing you good news, telling you to turn from these worthless things to the living God' " (vv. 14-15).

Actually, the apostles faced *two* dangers at Lystra. One was the worship and praise of people. The second was the wrath and persecution of the same people. "Then some Jews came from Antioch and Iconium and won the crowd over. They stoned Paul and dragged him outside the city, thinking he was dead" (v. 19). By far, the greatest of these dangers was the first. The apostles did not rend their garments when the people spoke of stoning them. They did, however, when the people wanted to worship them. Paul and Barnabas feared human worship more than their persecution, and rightly so.

Some time ago I heard a Christian leader tell of the subtleties of pride in his own life. When the mission director came with the missionary's immediate supervisor to visit him at his station, he would put on an air of super spirituality. He might have been sitting around reading a newsmagazine; but when his leaders came, he would hide the magazine and pretend to be reading his Bible. He practiced this deceit in order to get a good report card. He wanted them to leave his area singing his praises. But Scripture says we are to minister "not only to win their favor when their eye is on you, but like slaves of Christ, doing the will of God from your heart" (Eph. 6:6).

People seem especially vulnerable to the sin of seeking to glorify self in three areas, each involving something commendable and good in itself. The first is in our giving. Pastors may seek to impress others in their denominations with the size of the missionary budget of their church. Sunday School teachers may try to outdo other classes in the church so that their performance will go on the records and be seen by all. People may give generously to certain causes so that their names will appear on a special list or so that some leader might find out about it and drop them a personal note.

Jesus said,

> Be careful not to do your "acts of righteousness" before men, to be seen by them. If you do, you will have no reward from your Father in heaven. So when you give to the needy, do not announce it with trumpets, as the hypocrites do in the synagogues and on the streets, to be honored by men. I tell you the truth, they have received their reward in full. But when you give to the needy, do not let your left hand know what your right hand is doing, so that your giving may be in secret. Then your Father, who sees what is done in secret, will reward you (Matt. 6:1-4).

The second area in which leaders must guard their motives is in their production for the Lord. Annual denominational reports that tell of the successes of certain pastors in "adding to the flock" can be deadly. Pastors who are doing well can find themselves hoping that "Mr. Big" will see the statistics and be impressed. Remember two things in this. First, it is the Lord who adds to the church. "And the Lord added to their number daily those who were being saved" (Acts 2:47). Second, pride may lead to a fall. David got caught up in the sin of numbering the people, and that which he thought would bring him joy brought him heartache. "So the Lord sent a plague on Israel, and seventy thousand men of Israel fell dead" (1 Chron. 21:14).

The Lord has sent us forth as laborers, and as such He expects us to do what we can to further the message that will bring people into the kingdom. And the more the better. God is pleased when our labors are used by the Spirit of God to populate heaven and add to the number of disciples. But let's make sure we do it "as to the Lord and not unto men."

The third danger area for pride is in our service for Christ. Paul says, "I served the Lord with great humility and with tears" (Acts 20:19). He was serving God, not people. It is easy to slip into the sin of doing our best when someone important is watching and will commend us, but let things slide when just ordinary folks are around.

My wife is a constant challenge to me in this regard. The way she sets the table is a classic example. She does it the same way for family as she does for company. Occasionally we will have a missionary or a Christian leader in for dinner. She puts on no airs on their behalf. Whether guests are present or not, there is always a centerpiece. Peanut butter, jelly, jam, pickles, mustard, catsup, olives, relish—anything she serves is always presented tastefully in a serving dish rather than from the jar or bottle. Milk does not come to the table in a carton. The table never looks like a junkyard filled with jars, boxes, and bottles. The napkins and silverware are placed properly whether for company or just family. She never just "throws it on." She keeps our home as unto the Lord and tries to do her best for Him at all times (not as a pattern for others, but as a personal conviction).

Discouragement

The third deadly danger to the leader is discouragement. The devil is a master at causing this. Far too many leaders have been driven from their works in the depths of despair. Things haven't gone right, plans have fallen apart, critics have constantly reminded them of their shortcomings. People they thought they could count on either didn't carry their load or turned against them.

How does a leader handle this problem? We all face it. No

one is immune. It's rather surprising to see the record of Scripture concerning people of God caught up in the web of discouragement.

In Elijah's case, discouragement followed a great victory. That, by the way, is a rather common occurrence. A triumph is often followed by an emotional letdown or discouragement of some kind. Elijah had just prevailed spectacularly over the prophets of Baal on Mount Carmel. Baal's prophets had prayed, gashed themselves with knives, and cried out all day, but to no avail. They got no answers; their altar remained unlit. Then Elijah prayed a mighty prayer of faith, and God answered in such an unmistakable, fiery way that the people fell on their faces and said, "The Lord—He is God! The Lord—He is God!" (1 Kings 18:39)

Then things started to fall apart. Jezebel, the queen, heard what had happened. She sent a message to Elijah saying she was going to kill him. Having someone mad at you can be discouraging, especially if that person is evil and powerful like Jezebel. Elijah fled for his life.

Four lessons emerge from the results of discouragement in this story. First, discouragement brings a false sense of values. "He himself went a day's journey into the desert. He came to a broom tree, sat down under it and prayed that he might die. 'I have had enough, Lord,' he said. 'Take my life; I am no better than my ancestors.' Then he lay down under the tree and fell asleep" (19:4-5). What Elijah said in effect was, "We've all got to die sometime, so why not now. I am no different from anyone else, and since I'm going to die eventually, why not now?" But he was wrong. Elijah did not die—ever—for God had other plans for him. Years later, in God's time "a chariot of fire and horses of fire appeared and separated the two of them, and Elijah went up to heaven in a whirlwind" (2 Kings 2:11).

Second, discouragement can cause us to run from our responsibilities. "There he went into a cave and spent the night. And the word of the Lord came to him: 'What are you doing here, Elijah?' " (1 Kings 19:9) Leaders can begin to look around and conclude that the grass is greener on the other side of the fence. They can give up the work that God has assigned them. If they give up or run out on people who are looking to them for leadership, God is likely to come to them and say, "What are you doing here? Your place is in the job I gave you."

Third, discouragement can cause people to begin to blame others for their predicament. They can start pointing their finger at people around them and denounce them for their troubles. "He replied, 'I have been very zealous for the Lord God Almighty. The Israelites have rejected Your covenant, broken down Your altars, and put Your prophets to death with the sword. I am the only one left, and now they are trying to kill me too' " (v. 10). It's all their fault.

Fourth, discouragement can cause the leader to blow things completely out of perspective. Elijah cried out that he was the only man in the whole realm who had remained faithful to God. But the Lord said, "Not quite." He stated, "Yet I reserve seven thousand in Israel—all whose knees have not bowed down to Baal and all whose mouths have not kissed him" (v. 18). Things were dark and bleak for Elijah as he looked at them through the situation as he saw it. But the facts were completely different. Things were actually seven thousand times better than he thought.

Most of us can testify to the reality of that experience. When we are in the midst of a problem, nothing seems to turn out right. But things are rarely what they seem during those bleak days. When the fog lifts and the storm clears, we see a bit more clearly and things are often about seven thousand times better than they appeared.

David had a similar experience. He had left his city unprotected, and when he returned, it had been burned and the women and children taken captive (1 Sam. 30:3). The reaction of David and his men was normal: "So David and his men wept aloud until they had no strength left to weep" (v. 4). So here we find David caught up in sorrow and despair.

At that point an almost unbelievable thing happened. David's men, his comrades-in-arms, men who had followed him through thick and thin, spoke of stoning him. The one thing that David has always been able to rely on when everything else fell apart was the loyalty of these men. On more than one occasion they had risked their lives for him. That which he knew he could count on was no longer there. He was alone.

This forced David to turn to the one Person who was always near. He "found strength in the Lord his God" (v. 6). The Lord told him to pursue his ancient enemy and the final outcome was beautiful. David recovered all that the Amalekites had carried away. "Nothing was missing: young or old, boy or girl, plunder or anything else they had taken. David brought everything back" (v. 19).

In spite of the fact that things had never looked worse, the facts were that things were never better. Their wives and children were unhurt. His city had been burned, but *he was not going to need it anymore.* His kingdom was being prepared for him. Saul had died in battle, and David was about to be ushered into the palace. Had they known the facts when things looked their worst, they would have been rejoicing. They would have sung praises to God rather than lifting up their voices and weeping "until they had no strength left to weep."

Discouragement often has that effect. Problems can be blown completely out of perspective. Molehills become mountains. The leader must continue to walk by faith and wait till the picture clears. The Apostle Paul is a pacesetter in this. His arrival in Philippi had been followed by trouble and discouragement. But as he looked back, he was able to say, "Now I want you to know, brothers, that what has happened to me has really served to advance the Gospel" (Phil. 1:12).

Three things then can be the downfall of a leader: A covetous heart, a craving for self-glory, or discouragement. The enemy of our souls has been using these in the lives of men and women since Adam and Eve fell. There is no human defense against them. Satan knows how to circumvent, sweep aside, and destroy our human defenses.

But God wants to deliver us and will if we trust Him. As an old man, David could look back over his years of experience with God and say, "Yours, O Lord, is the greatness and the power and the glory and the majesty and the splendor, for everything in heaven and earth is Yours. . . . Now, our God, we give You thanks, and praise Your glorious name" (1 Chron. 29:11, 13).

Chapter Eleven

Meeting the Needs of the Group

One of the prime goals of Christian leaders should be the deepening of the spiritual lives of the people they lead. These people must grow in grace and in the knowledge of Christ, developing in their effectiveness for Him and deepening in their devotion. It is God's desire that they demonstrate Christlike qualities in everyday life.

The Bible is alive with examples of this. Under David's leadership the men around him won battle after battle, defending the kingdom against the enemies of God. But the greatest accomplishments were in the lives of the men themselves.

How were these men described when they came to David? "All those who were in distress or in debt or discontented gathered around him, and he became their leader. About four hundred men were with him" (1 Sam. 22:2).

Later, after lengthy association with David, these men became strong, dedicated, mighty men of valor. Scripture describes one of them, Eleazar, as

one of the three mighty men . . . with David when they taunted the Philistines gathered at Pas Dammim for battle. . . . He stood his ground and struck down the Philistines till his hand grew tired and froze to the sword. The Lord brought about a great victory that day. The troops returned to Eleazar, but only to strip the dead (2 Sam. 23:9-10).

"It Takes One to Make One"

The influence of leaders on their associates is an interesting thing to observe throughout the Bible. For instance, how many giant-killers were in Saul's army? None. When Goliath defied the armies of God, they quaked with fear (see 1 Sam. 17:11). David, who came to bring food to his brothers, sized up the situation, went out in faith, and killed the giant.

After David, the giant killer, became king, how many giant killers arose in Israel? Quite a few. They were almost a common commodity in the army under David's leadership.

> At that time Sibbecai the Hushathite killed Sippai, one of the descendants of the Rephaites, and the Philistines were subjugated. In another battle with the Philistines, Elhanan son of Jair killed Lahmi the brother of Goliath the Gittite, who had a spear with a shaft like a weaver's rod. In still another battle, which took place at Gath, there was a huge man with six fingers on each hand and six toes on each foot—twenty-four in all. He also was descended from Rapha. When he taunted Israel, Jonathan son of Shimea, David's brother, killed him. These were descendants of Rapha in Gath, and they fell at the hands of David and his men (1 Chron. 20:4-8).

Why do you suppose there were no giant killers in Saul's army? One reason, I'm sure, was because Saul himself was not one. However, under David's leadership they were numerous. Why? Because David was one. This illustrates a tremendous principle of leadership, a principle which runs throughout the Bible. *It takes one to make one.*

Our Lord's last command was "go, make disciples among all nations." Naturally, the command was not given to the multitudes but to the eleven men—His disciples. Why? *It takes one to make one.*

Therefore, if you are going to see strong, devoted disciples of Christ raised up under your leadership, you yourself must be one. *It takes one to make one.*

More on that later. But for now, let's ask how we go about this task. What can we do to see men and women of God raised up to serve Him?

It will become obvious to you as you lead that not all of the members of your group have the same devotion and desire to grow. Some are more eager and dedicated than others. This simple fact requires that you figure out a way to keep the interest and motivation of each person high and at the same time help those who are more on fire to develop to the maximum. Let us suggest a two-point program.

Voluntary Study Groups

First, arrange a special volunteer Bible study and prayer group. I have found this to be of tremendous value. Here are a few tips that may help you get a group started.

When you detect a special hunger and interest on the part of a few people, go to them privately and ask if they would be interested in meeting for Bible study and prayer at an early morning hour some day each week.

The advantages of meeting early in the morning are twofold. First, it avoids taking an evening. People don't generally need one more evening taken up with something. Quite often they are gone from their families too much already. Second, the early hour eliminates the halfhearted. Only the most dedicated will rise a couple hours early one day each week. After you have three or four people "signed up," announce this special Bible study and prayer time to the entire group. Invite anyone who wants to join you to do so. No one can then accuse you of playing favorites, of showing more interest in and giving more time to certain ones. Make your invitation "come one, come all — everybody welcome!"

As a matter of fact, you will probably be surprised at who comes. Often a deep fire burns in the soul of one who shows little outward evidence. Tell them that the rules and standards of the group will be decided on at a breakfast meeting the coming week. That's important. The specifics of how you spend your time should be discussed and decided together within the framework of some working principles that you lay out for them in line with your objectives.

When you meet at breakfast to make plans, begin by telling them the purpose you have in mind. A few well-selected Scripture verses will help clarify some specific goals and give your presentation some punch and authority. A few passages that I have found helpful follow. I have shared various of these with different groups, depending on their level of maturity and depth of interests.

Romans 8:29: "For those God foreknew He also predestined to be conformed to the likeness of His Son, that He might be the firstborn among many brothers." Goal: to become more like Jesus.

John 5:39: "You diligently study the Scriptures because you think that by them you possess eternal life. These are the Scriptures that testify about Me." Goal: to learn more about Jesus.

Acts 20:32: "Now I commit you to God and to the word of His grace, which can build you up and give you an inheritance among all those who are sanctified." Goal: to be built up in the Word of God.

Matthew 9:36-38: "When He saw the crowds, He had compassion on them, because they were harassed and helpless, like sheep without a shepherd. Then He said to His disciples, 'The harvest is plentiful but the workers are few. Ask the Lord of the harvest, therefore, to send out workers into His harvest field.' " Goal: to spend time praying that God will raise up laborers for the harvest fields of the world.

Psalm 119:9, 11: "How can a young man keep his way pure? By living according to Your Word. . . . I have hidden Your Word in my heart that I might not sin against You." Goal: to memorize Scripture—for clean lives.

Psalm 119:105: "Your Word is a lamp to my feet and a light for my path." Goal: to apply the Scriptures as our light and lamp—for guidance.

Jeremiah 33:3: "Call to Me and I will answer you and tell you great and unsearchable things you do not know." Goal: to pray for specific needs in our lives.

Hebrews 11:6: "And without faith it is impossible to please God, because anyone who comes to Him must believe that He exists and that He rewards those who earnestly seek Him." Goal: to deepen our faith.

Select a Bible study program for the group to use. One that has been used with great profit by groups around the world is "Design for Discipleship," a six-booklet Bible study program developed for either individual or group use. It can be ordered from The Navigators, P.O. Box 6000, Colorado Springs, CO 80934.

Many other excellent Bible study guides are available through your Christian bookstore. *Disciples Are Made — Not Born* by Walt Henrichsen, *Know Why You Believe* and *Know What You Believe* by Paul Little, *What Did Jesus Say About That?* by Stanley C. Baldwin are all good, to name just a few.

Assign a chapter for discussion the following week. Have each person complete his or her study before coming to the study group. This ensures a lively Bible-based discussion when you meet. You might want to make a phone call sometime during the week to each member of the group to see how they are coming on their study. A personal contact by phone and time spent in prayer for each of them will be used of God to stimulate faithfulness and desire on their part.

When you meet, allow adequate time for prayer. One early morning group that I led for a year had a strong personal witnessing outreach as one of its objectives. This prompted us to pray along the specific lines of evangelism. We based our prayer time on four passages of Scripture:

Colossians 4:2-4: "Devote yourselves to prayer, being watchful and thankful. And pray for us, too, that God may open a door for our message, so that we may proclaim the mystery of Christ, for which I am in chains. Pray that I may proclaim it clearly, as I should." In this passage Paul prays for an open door to speak the mystery of Christ. In our group we made a list of people and began praying that God would open an opportunity to witness to them. We made these people specific subjects of personal daily prayer as well as praying for them together in the group.

Acts 16:14 speaks of Lydia: "The Lord opened her heart to respond to Paul's message." We made a list of people to whom we had witnessed and who seemed to show some interest, and prayed that God would open their hearts.

Colossians 1:9-10: "For this reason, since the day we heard about you, we have not stopped praying for you and asking God to fill you with the knowledge of His will through all spiritual wisdom and understanding. And we pray this in order that you may live a life worthy of the Lord and may please Him in every way: bearing fruit in every good work, growing in the knowledge of God." We made a list of each person who came to Christ through our witness and prayed for their growth and maturity in Christ.

Matthew 9:36-38: "When He saw the crowds, He had compassion on them, because they were harassed and helpless, like sheep without a shepherd. Then He said to His disciples, 'The harvest is plentiful but the workers are few. Ask the Lord of the harvest, therefore, to send out workers into His harvest field.' " We made no list from these verses but simply prayed that God would raise up laborers in our midst.

If your group is highly motivated to learn the Word of God, a plan of Scripture memory can be incorporated. Decide how many Scripture verses you will memorize each week, and spend about five minutes of your time together in checking each other on your verses. The group can pair off by twos, each person quoting his or her verses to the other person. Memorize the reference with the verse and strive for word perfection. The Navigator's Topical Memory System has been used by Christians all over the world. It can be ordered from The Navigators.

Personal Time

The second part of your program to keep the highly motivated growing toward spiritual maturity is similar to the first but more intense.

After you have had your study group for a few months, it will become evident to you that one or two members of the group are growing faster and showing greater spiritual hunger than the others. These are the ones you have been waiting for! God is preparing them for greater use in His kingdom. Go to these people personally and ask if they would like to meet on a personal basis—person to person—for some special training. Explain that you would like to have lunch with them to explain fully what you have in mind.

God has spoken to my own heart about this phase of leadership from Isaiah 58:10: "And if you spend yourselves on behalf of the hungry and satisfy the needs of the oppressed, then your light will rise in the darkness, and your night will become like the noonday." When I observe a person who has a special hunger to learn the Scriptures and grow in grace, I must be willing to share my life with that person and pass along those things that God has taught me.

Paul also spoke of this:

You are witnesses, and so is God, of how holy, righteous and blameless we were among you who believed. For you know that we dealt with each of you as a father deals with his own children, encouraging, comforting and urging you to live lives worthy of God, who calls you into His kingdom and glory (1 Thes. 2:10-11).

Note the phrase "as a father deals with his own children." How does a father train his children? Always on an individual basis! My daughter has a completely different set of interests and needs from those of my son. I must make time for each of them individually to discuss the issues of life they are facing at the time.

The concept of the leader spending time individually with his or her key person is as old as the concept of leadership itself. Moses prayed that God would give him someone to be his successor.

Moses said to the Lord, "May the Lord, the God of the spirits of all mankind, appoint a man over this community

to go out and come in before them, one who will lead
them out and bring them in, so the Lord's people will not
be like sheep without a shepherd" (Num. 27:15-17).

Later the Lord instructed Moses: "But commission Joshua,
and encourage and strengthen him, for he will lead this people
across and will cause them to inherit the land that you will
see" (Deut. 3:28). Note that God assigned Moses the task of
charging, encouraging, and *strengthening* Joshua. This was a
person-to-person ministry.

As you compare this command of Moses with 1 Thessalonians 2:12 (encouraging, comforting, and urging) and 1 Corinthians 14:3 ("But everyone who prophesies speaks to men for
their strengthening, encouragement and comfort"), an interesting pattern emerges. This gives us a great deal of guidance
as to what to do with those with whom we will meet individually. I try to include four things during these times together.

1. Edification: share things with them that will edify and build
them up in the faith. Make your training time a positive thing.
Build upon their strengths. Encourage them to develop their
gifts.

2. Exhortation: from time to time it is necessary to point out
areas in a person's life that need to be brought back into line
with the Word of God.

3. Comfort: help them with the things that are bugging them.
Encourage them when they are down. Help them meet their
problems.

4. Charge: assign them special projects that will help meet
specific needs in their lives or build on their gifts and abilities.
Begin to familiarize yourself with devotional booklets and guides
that you can give them to read and discuss with you later.

Through these special times with you the life of these people will be tremendously affected. But another thing will occur.

Others in the group will notice their growth, greater dedication, and greater familiarity with the Scriptures. This will prompt a hunger on their part and a desire to experience the same thing.

Some years ago I had the responsibility of leading a Sunday evening church youth group. I began to share with them the principles of spiritual growth and Christian maturity.

After a couple of months, one young man named Jerry developed a real hunger for the things of God. He would corner me from time to time and ask questions that revealed a heart that was very tender toward the Lord.

I suggested we meet for special prayer and study on Sunday morning before Sunday School. He had a paper route and finished up about 8:30 in the morning. So that's when we met. I got him into personal Bible study and Scripture memory, and he began to have a daily quiet time with the Lord.

Jerry grew like a weed. Soon others in the class noticed this and began to inquire what was going on in Jerry's life. When we explained, others wanted to get in on it. Soon we had a hard core of kids who were showing many of the characteristics of true discipleship.

Jerry began to help another guy, and soon the process of multiplication was operating throughout the group. The idea is contained in 2 Timothy 2:2: "And the things you have heard me say in the presence of many witnesses entrust to reliable men who will also be qualified to teach others."

When I begin meeting with a person to train him or her in godly living and effective outreach, am I satisfied when that person comes to me and tells me he or she has led someone to Christ?

No, I'm happy but not satisfied. I want that person not only to be able to lead someone to Christ, but also to pass along to that other person the principles of Christian growth.

When he or she begins to do that am I satisfied?

No, I'm happy but not satisfied. I want that person to stick with the other person until he or she in turn is used of God to lead another person to Christ.

Am I now satisfied?

No, I want that person in turn to be able to repeat the process with a new person.

Am I satisfied now? Yes, because that will be clear evidence to me that the person I originally helped has fully caught the idea.

Let me illustrate. Let's say I help Pete in his Christian life, and one day he leads Joe to Christ. I now know that Pete has been brought to the place of maturity where he can lead a person to Christ, but I still don't know whether he knows how to follow that person up.

It is not until Joe begins to mature and eventually leads someone to Christ that I know for sure that Pete knows how to train Joe to lead a person to Christ and follow him up to the point where he can go and do likewise. So it's when Joe comes to Pete and says, "I've led someone to Christ" that I know my training of Pete has been effective.

In this case it was LeRoy to Pete to Joe to Sam. So until I see Sam, I'm not sure that I'm really getting through to Pete. If you can grasp that idea, it will make your leadership effective and productive beyond your wildest dreams. Meditate for a while on 2 Timothy 2:2. Ask God to multiply your life.

Chapter Twelve

Communication

Communication is a vital part of leadership. Leaders must frequently be in front of people. They may have to make announcements, teach lessons, introduce speakers, or give short talks. In one capacity or another they will be trying to get something across to others.

How do you get ready? What do you do to put your ideas together so that they make sense to your listeners? Are there any general rules to follow that will help you accomplish your objective? Let me begin by sharing a personal experience.

My wife and I were walking down the street of a small town in Iowa one Sunday morning forty years ago. I had a job with the railroad, which took me away from home frequently to various towns on the line, and Virginia had come to spend the weekend with me. We were at loose ends with nothing to do, and as we walked along we heard church bells.

Sort of as a joke I said, "Let's go to church."

She was a bit surprised and said, "What for?"

"Oh, I don't know," I answered, "lots of people do that sort of thing, and we don't have anything to do 'til lunch time."

"OK," she said, "where shall we go?"

"I don't care. How about that one over there?" I pointed to one across the street.

So we went in and sat down. Naturally we felt a little out of place, but we settled down to see what would happen. We were in for the surprise of our lives. When the minister gave the sermon, both of us became keenly interested. It wasn't his subject matter—though later we knew that he had preached the Gospel. What drew our interest was the *way* he did it. Two things stood out: you could tell that he knew what he was talking about, and he meant what he said.

Virginia and I had been to church before and had heard other preachers. But this was the first minister who had these two qualities. Some we had heard seemed to know what they were talking about, but spoke with no conviction—they didn't seem to mean it. Others meant what they said, but didn't seem to know what they were talking about.

Imperatives in Speaking

As I've reflected on that incident over the years, these two things have stood out more and more as vital in speaking.

First, *know your subject.* To establish confidence in the minds of your listeners, you must study and prepare carefully. Do your homework. If your audience realizes that you really have a grasp of your topic and that you are only sharing a part of all that you know, it gives them a sense of confidence and trust. They believe you.

Second, *say it like you mean it.* Naturally, the first leads into the second. You must be convinced in your own mind before others will be convinced. This is one of the things that made Jesus' ministry outstanding. It was said of Him that He spoke "as One who had authority, and not as their teachers of the law" (Matt. 7:29). The scribes were like schoolboys reciting a lesson; Jesus spoke with an authority and conviction that astounded His listeners.

Another incident in the New Testament bears witness to this truth. Paul and Barnabas, while ministering in Iconium, "went as usual into the Jewish synagogue. There they spoke so effectively that a great number of Jews and Gentiles believed" (Acts 14:1).

Ponder those words *they spoke so effectively.* It was not only *what* they said; it was the way they said it.

The lesson is clear. The Holy Spirit is pointing out to us that the *manner* with which we get our message across has something to do with the reception it will get. A dull speaker, droning along in a monotonous voice, soon has you feeling sleepy. Well, believe me, the minister in that church many years ago did not put me to sleep. He held my attention. He knew what he was talking about! And he meant what he said!

Content in Messages

OK, you say, I'm convinced. But how do I go about putting together a talk that is both interesting and accomplishes something? As I have listened to speakers who communicate effectively, I have learned two things.

First, *preach the Word.* By that I do not mean that you give a Bible-based talk. More than that. Your talk must have Bible content. As you inject the Scriptures throughout, they give your message flavor and zest and power. The Holy Spirit takes His sword (see Eph. 6:17) to prick consciences and probe hearts. "The Word of God is living and active. Sharper than any double-edged sword, it penetrates even to dividing soul and spirit, joints and marrow; it judges the thoughts and attitudes of the heart" (Heb. 4:12).

The Holy Spirit takes the Word and uses it to break down walls of resistance to obedience and faith. " 'Is not My Word like fire,' declares the Lord, 'and like a hammer that breaks a rock in pieces?' " (Jer. 23:29) So be sure to salt your talk generously with the Word of God.

You learn the second important aspect of communication from the life of Jesus: *tell stories.* Use illustrations. Jesus was the master storyteller:

"No one ever spoke like this man."
"Behold, a sower went forth to sow."
"A woman had a coin."
"A man had two sons."
"The kingdom of God is like . . ."

Use your illustration or story to help your audience understand the point you are making and the Scripture you are using. Let me demonstrate.

I was asked to give a talk on how to get the Word of God into our lives. One of the points I made was that we must learn to meditate on the Scriptures: "Oh, how I love Your law! I meditate on it all day long" (Ps. 119:97). I shared this illustration:

If you were to come to our home in the evening, we would talk for a while, and then I might ask if you would like to see the rest of the house. As you started down to see the lower level, I could leave the lights off and hand you a birthday candle with which to look around. You would go from room to room and peer into the gloom, and soon you would return upstairs.

"What did you see?" I'd ask.

"Well, I saw a room with a Ping-Pong table, a family room, a bedroom off the hall, and a room that looked like a small den or library."

"Right!" I'd say. "That's what's down there all right."

Then we would both go down, turn on all the lights, make ourselves comfortable, and look around the family room. Soon it would become apparent that a real decorator worked on this room. You'd notice the careful balance of colors and furnishings. You'd see how the pictures on the walls were just right and blended in well with the colors in the rug and furniture. Question: Did you see the family room with the birthday candle? Answer: Yes. But did you *really* see it as it is? No, you really saw it when we turned on all the lights, sat down, and took the time to let the beauty of the room come through.

This illustrates the difference between reading the Word and meditating on the Word. Often reading the Word can be like hurrying through the house with a birthday candle, glancing here and there, catching a glimpse of this and that. But the richness of the Word—its depth and beauty and wonder and majesty—only comes as we take the time to sit with it, ponder it in our minds, and let the Holy Spirit reveal its depths to us.

So then, here's the pattern:

1. State the point: Meditate on the Word.

2. State the Scripture: Psalm 119:97.

3. Give an illustration: The birthday candle story—to show the difference between reading and meditation.

If you have a talk that has three or four points, you repeat the process three or four times. After you give a brief introduction to your theme, you make your points. For example:

How to Fill Our Lives with the Word
I. Study the Word
   A. Scripture—Proverbs 2:1-5; Acts 17:11
   B. Illustration—A man searching for treasure must dig deep; he rarely finds his precious metal lying around on top of the ground.
II. Memorize the Word
   A. Scripture—Colossians 3:16; Proverbs 7:1-3; Deuteronomy 6:6-7.
   B. Illustration—The Vietnam prisoners-of-war who had memorized God's Word were able to use it to enable them to survive the rigors of the Hanoi Hilton and help other men as well.
III. Meditate on the Word
   A. Scripture—Psalm 119:97; Psalm 1:2-3; Joshua 1:8
   B. Illustration—The birthday candle story.
IV. Closing application
   Show a method of Scripture memory or Bible study they can use day by day on their own.

Notice that throughout the message the Scriptures are central. A story or illustration adds a bit of spark and illumination. At the end a practical application shows the group how to do something about it. Try this approach each time you give a talk. Speakers often challenge and exhort us, leaving us with the desire to follow through. But they say nothing about *how* we could do it. A leader must be practical and provide the "how-to."

When you use a story or illustration, be sure to select one to which your audience can relate. A wheat farmer in Kansas would see things differently from a factory worker in New Jersey.

We have not all bumped our heads on the same brick wall.

An illustration I once used in Singapore is a classic example of how not to do it. In trying to make my point, I told a story of two guys in Nevada who almost froze to death in a driving snowstorm. My audience had never heard of Nevada, had never seen snow, and couldn't imagine anyone freezing to death. I would have been far better off talking about the three Hebrew youths in the burning, fiery furnace. Singapore, after all, *is* hot!

Overcoming Nervousness

A major obstacle to overcome in speaking is nervousness. I know—I have this problem. In fact, whether I'm witnessing to one person or speaking to a group, I find that my throat gets dry and my hands get wet. I wish it were the other way around, but it never is. A verse that comforts me in regard to this problem is "But in your hearts acknowledge Christ as the holy Lord. Always be prepared to give an answer to everyone who asks you to give the reason for the hope that you have. But do this with gentleness and respect" (1 Peter 3:15-16).

Notice Peter says, "With gentleness and respect." So if you feel a bit fearful, rejoice! You qualify! If God wanted us to be brash and to have the feeling we are well-qualified in our own intellect and strength, He would have said so. But when the butterflies begin to rise in our stomachs, our hands begin to shake, our knees begin to knock, and our throats get dry, that's when we find ourselves on our knees before God asking for His grace and strength. And that's when He can use us.

> But He said to me, "My grace is sufficient for you, for My power is made perfect in weakness." Therefore, I will boast all the more gladly about my weaknesses, so that Christ's power may rest on me. That is why, for Christ's sake, I delight in weaknesses, in insults, in hardships, in persecutions, in difficulties. For when I am weak, then I am strong (2 Cor. 12:9-10).

Often I have to speak to an unfriendly audience. My talk might be in a college dorm or classroom or in a meeting in the student union. Usually some students come to the meeting to try to prove I am wrong and who object to the message of the Gospel. I've learned a couple of things the hard way that help overcome nervousness.

First, when you are giving a message that sticks to the Word of God, you have an advantage that should give you the boldness of Daniel. That advantage is this: *what you are saying is true.* Whether people believe it or not doesn't change the fact. Jesus said, "Your Word is truth" (John 17:17). Paul spoke of "the Word of truth, the Gospel" (Col. 1:5). In a world where the only constant is change, it is a blessed thing to know that your message, the Word of God, is eternal Truth.

> For you have been born again, not of perishable seed, but of imperishable, through the living and enduring word of God. For, "all men are like grass, and all their glory is like the wild flower; the grass withers, and the flower falls, but the word of the Lord stands forever." And this is the Word that was preached to you (1 Peter 1:23-25).

Second, it helps to *smile.* The shortest distance between two people is a friendly smile. It sort of takes the edge off your nervousness and their hostility. As I said, this is one of those things I learned the hard way.

Lorne Sanny, Walt Henrichsen, and I were in the Pacific Northwest on a ministry trip. When we arrived at Oregon State University, I was amazed to see huge signs across the length of the high-rise dormitories reading, "LeRoy is coming." Immediately fear gripped me. I just knew that at our meeting that night a gang would be waiting to skin me alive. When LeRoy came, they'd be waiting.

The meeting was held in a large classroom and there was a good turnout. I arrived feeling nervous and apprehensive as to the outcome. The emcee got the meeting started and turned it over to me. I looked over the audience and noted what seemed to be a sinister pocket of bushy-haired radicals. So I grimly began my presentation—unsmiling—and laid it out hard and clear. To my amazement they listened with great interest, and when we opened up for questions, theirs were honest and sincere.

After the meeting ended, they came up to the front, shook hands, and said, "Praise the Lord, Brother! It's sure great to hear the Gospel presented so clearly. Thank you for coming." For the first time all night I smiled.

On the way home Lorne said to me, "You should have smiled once in a while. It would have helped give the meeting a little warmth." I knew he was right and learned another valuable lesson.

The Major Ingredient

Prayer is an essential part of message preparation and presentation. Pray before you begin to prepare and pray before you make your presentation. Pray that the Holy Spirit will give you the right Scriptures and illustrations and that He will enable you to give the message under His power.

This was another one of those lessons I learned the hard way. For two years in the mid '50s, I was on a team that presented the Gospel to fraternities and sororities at the University of Pittsburgh and at Carnegie Tech. We would go in on Monday evenings, present the Gospel, make appointments, and then talk to these individuals during the week.

One of the things we decided at the outset was to pray together before each meeting. We were working with Campus Crusade for Christ at the time, and Bill Bright of Crusade had urged us to spend much time on our knees with God before we went to each meeting. The Lord laid on our hearts the necessity of this prayer time, and we were faithful to it. The Lord blessed our efforts, and soon we had quite a large number of new converts whom we were leading in Bible study. Some of them in turn were going to other fraternities and giving their testimonies as part of our team. Things were going well.

I suppose we became complacent or proud or overconfident or something, but our prayer time began to grow lax. Then one night it happened. I was busy, and the rest of the team had things to do. So we met at the fraternity house where we were to speak, out of breath and in a rush. One of us offered a hasty sentence prayer, and we hurried into the meeting.

I could tell from the moment the meeting started it was going to be a disaster. The emcee couldn't get proper attention. The men who gave their testimonies sounded like robots giving a stock market report. When I stood up to speak, there was absolutely no sense of the presence of the Holy Spirit ministering to hearts. It was a canned speech and nothing more. When we closed the meeting, they politely hustled us out of the house.

We looked at each other and knew what we had to do. We got into our car and spent a good deal of time in prayer, confessing our sin to God and asking His forgiveness. That was the last time we neglected our prayer time before the meeting. The Lord heard our prayers and continued to bless His Word. And through it all we learned a lesson we'll never forget.

"Not that we are competent to claim anything for ourselves, but our competence comes from God. He has made us competent as ministers of a new covenant—not of the letter but of the Spirit; for the letter kills, but the Spirit gives life" (2 Cor. 3:5-6). "I can do everything through Him who gives me strength" (Phil. 4:13).

Other Books by LeRoy Eims

Be a Motivational Leader. LeRoy Eims shows how to maintain high motivation and morale within a group, equipping people to be and do their best for Christ. For church, home, business, and community leaders. Textbook 6-3512 with Personal and Group Study Guide.

Personal and Group Study Guide

For Personal Study

Settle into your favorite chair with your Bible, a pen or pencil, and this book. Read a chapter, marking portions that seem significant to you. Write in the margins. Note where you agree, disagree, or question the author. Look up relevant Scripture passages. Then turn to the questions listed in this study guide. If you want to trace your progress with a written record, use a notebook to record your answers, thoughts, feelings, and further questions. Refer to the text and to the Scriptures as you allow the questions to enlarge your thinking. And pray. Ask God to give you a discerning mind for truth, an active concern for others, and a greater love for Him.

For Group Study

Plan ahead. Before meeting with your group, read and mark the chapter as if you were preparing for personal study. Glance through the questions making mental notes of how you might contribute to your group's discussion. Bring a Bible and the text to your meeting.

Arrange an environment that promotes discussion. Comfortable chairs arranged in a casual circle invite people to talk with each other. It says, "We are here to listen and respond to each other—and to learn together." If you are the leader, simply be sure to sit where you can have eye contact with each person.

Promptness counts. Time is as valuable to many people as money. If the group runs late (because of a late start), these people will feel as robbed as if you had picked their pockets. So unless you have mutual agreement, begin and end on time.

Involve everyone. Group learning works best if everyone participates more or less equally. If you are a natural *talker,* pause before you enter the conversation. Then ask a quiet person what he or she thinks. If you are a natural *listener,* don't hesitate to jump into the discussion. Others will benefit from your thoughts but only if you speak to them. If you are the *leader,* be careful not to dominate the session. Of course, you will have thought about the study ahead of time, but don't assume that people are present just to hear you—as flattering as that may feel. Instead, help group members make their own discoveries. Ask the questions, but insert your own ideas only as they are needed to fill gaps.

Pace the study. The questions for each session are designed to last about one hour. Early questions form the framework for later discussion. So don't rush by so quickly that you miss a valuable foundation. Later questions, however, often speak of the here and now. So don't dawdle so long at the beginning that you leave no time to "get personal." While the leader must take responsibility for timing the flow of questions, it is the job of each person in the group to assist in keeping the study moving at an even pace.

Pray for each other—together and alone. Then watch God's hand at work in all of your lives.

Notice that each session includes the following features:

Session Topic—a brief statement summarizing the session.

Community Builder—an activity to get acquainted with the session topic and/or with each other.

Discovery Questions—a list of questions to encourage individual or group discovery and application.

Prayer Focus—suggestions for turning one's learning into prayer.

Optional Activities—supplemental ideas that will enhance the study.

Assignment—activities or preparation to complete prior to the next session.

One

Who Is Fit to Lead?

Session Topic
God accomplishes His purposes by using leaders who will respond to His call regardless of their feelings of inadequacy.

Community Builder
1. Why are you interested in studying this book?
2. Think of a spiritual leader who you know personally and think highly of. What do you believe has made this person fit to lead?

Discovery Questions
1. Which people or positions do you think of when you hear the word *leader*?
2. What do you think are some essential qualifications for a person who leads?
3. What (if anything) do you think might disqualify a person from leadership?
4. When a voice spoke to Moses from the burning bush, Moses was certain it was God. Eims states that when you need to make a decision, you must, like Moses, make certain that God is in it before doing anything. To what extent do you operate this way?
5. If God is truly able and willing to show His will for us, why does it sometimes seem difficult to discern God's will?
6. What does Eims claim is "one of the great secrets of leadership in the Christian enterprise" (p. 11)?
7. How do you feel about the argument between Moses and God?
8. How has one of your own weaknesses actually proved to be a strength? (See 1 Cor. 12:7-10.)

9. What were the objections of Moses, Gideon, and Jeremiah to God's call?

10. What would be your own objections if God were to call you to a significant position of leadership?

11. What kinds of leadership situations do you try to avoid? Why?

12. Describe a situation where a person might not yet be ready for a position of leadership?

13. What place do you think education or training ought to have in preparation for Christian leadership?

Prayer Focus

* Give thanks to the Lord for His absolute sufficiency and for the opportunity to be a person He uses to accomplish His plan and purposes. Pray that God will increase your faith in the fact that He and His strength are always with you and working through you.

Optional Activities

1. Search your heart for any pride in yourself because of your family background, education or training, social skills, speaking ability, a job offer, or other experience. Discuss how these things relate to Eims' concept that when God calls a person to lead, "it doesn't matter who you are."

2. Read several times and consider memorizing 2 Corinthians 3:4-5 and 12:9-10.

Assignment

1. Read chapter 2 and work through the study.

2. Think about God's power when you sense it working through you and what conditions seem to make that more likely.

T w o

The Leader's Source of Power

Session Topic
Fellowship with the Lord, drawn from Scripture, prayer, and obedience, is essential in order to lead others toward God.

Community Builder
1. When in your walk with God have you felt that the power was turned off? How did your fellowship with God continue?
2. Would you compare your own relationship with God more like a dimmer switch or an on/off switch? Using the power switch analogy, what do you think would be an ideal power structure for you? Consider long-life bulbs, solar-powered heat or fluorescent energy, surge suppressors, extension cords, and so on.

Discovery Questions
1. What blocks do you experience in your efforts to maintain vital fellowship with God? What Scripture passages address this problem?
2. Eims says that fellowship with God makes His power "operative and effective in our lives" (p. 18). What part does the Holy Spirit play in that connection?
3. Eims says on page 21 that we should have as our first priority "a life of intimate, personal, dynamic fellowship" with God. What are other priorities that might be competing for that first place?
4. What are some ways that we can measure if something is our first priority?
5. What role, if any, do you think your other daily activities play in shaping you more like the image of Jesus Christ?
6. Eims says that one of the three basic elements for a life

of fellowship with the Lord is the Word of God. How could you determine whether the time, study, or meditation you give to Scripture is adequate?

7. On page 24, Eims states that a person can pray "as a means to impress" or "to accomplish something." How can you tell the difference in your own praying?

8. What does it mean to pray without ceasing? (See 1 Thes. 5:17.)

9. What do you think of Eims' belief that for prayer to be fervent, it must be specific? (Can you think of any biblical examples of general prayers?)

10. What else might characterize fervent prayer besides being specific?

11. A life of obedience by the leader is a great motivation to people who follow. In our age of isolated lives, how can you help people notice your life of obedience to God?

12. The author suggests that three elements characterize those who fellowship with God: study of Scripture, prayer, and obedience. Which of these elements (or others) do you enjoy most in your fellowship with God? Explain.

Prayer Focus
* Pray that God will motivate you to seek a growing fellowship with Him.

Optional Activities
1. Ask a local spiritual leader to tell you how he or she maintains regular fellowship with God.

2. Make a specific plan for change in one of Eims' three areas of fellowship with God in which you most need improvement.

Assignment
1. Read chapter 3 of the text.

2. Reflect on what qualities of the inner life are important for a leader.

Three

The Inner Life of the Leader

Session Topic
Purity, humility, and faith are basic, essential qualities of the inner life of a leader.

Community Builder
1. As a group, list on a flip-chart the qualities of an ideal church leader. Agree on a certain leadership position if necessary (for example, pastor, elder, Sunday School superintendent, director of women's ministry). Put an asterisk by the qualities that are essential.

2. Assume you are the CEO of a retail sales company. As you interview potential employees for a management position, what qualities would you be looking for?

Discovery Questions
1. What is the connection, if any, between desirable outer qualities (such as those of Daniel and his friends, as listed on pp. 28-29) and the three inner qualities of purity, humility, and faith?

2. "Daniel resolved not to defile himself" (Dan. 1:8). What does the word "resolved" mean to you? What role does this play in purity?

3. When have you gone by the appearance of someone and later found out that you made a wrong assumption? Think of one example of thinking too positively and one of thinking too negatively.

4. On pages 32-33 Eims gives the "6–8–10 principles" of determining right from wrong in the gray areas. Choose something that is a gray area in your choices and apply the four principles to determine if it could be included in a life of purity.

Do you agree with the outcome? Why or why not?

5. Are there different standards of purity for leaders than for those not in leadership? Explain.

6. Eims stresses humility as a virtue for leaders. How can leaders recognize when they are focusing on themselves too much and falling into the trap of pride? What is the remedy for this?

7. Eims states that pride breeds two "dreadful diseases of the soul," ignorance and insecurity (p. 37). How have you seen these at work in your own life?

8. Most people would equate a proud spirit with overconfidence instead of insecurity. What do you think?

9. Name the four aspects of the meaning of faith recorded on pages 39-43. Which is the toughest one for you?

10. What are some ways a group of leaders working together could help each other develop and maintain a godly inner life?

Prayer Focus

* Dedicate your inner life to God and ask Him to mold you into a leader fit to serve such a great God. Ask Him to help you not judge people superficially but be able to see as He sees.

Optional Activities

1. Try to catch yourself this week making judgments based on the way someone appears.

2. Do an informal survey of two teens and two adults. Ask them which leaders they look up to most and why. Note whether their reasons are based on the outer or the inner life of the person.

Assignment

1. Read chapter 4 of the text and work through the study.

2. Notice your basic attitude toward others, focusing especially on your demonstration of a servant heart and/or a sensitive spirit.

Four

The Leader's Attitude toward Others

Session Topic
Two characteristics that are essential for a leader's attitude toward others are a servant heart and a sensitive spirit.

Community Builder
1. Imagine that you are the owner of a local, medium-sized restaurant. What could you do to demonstrate the servant attitude that Jesus modeled for us?

2. Now imagine that your job there is to "bus" the tables. How could you have a servant attitude in that situation?

Discovery Questions
1. What objections might you have or hear concerning the J–O–Y principle described on page 44? What makes people object to this principle?

2. In Mark 10:45 the *King James Version* uses the word "minister" where other versions use "serve." How might these two words give a different impression? Would you rather minister to or serve someone?

3. Philippians 2:3 says, "Let each of you regard one another as more important than himself" (NASB). Do you think that it is ever unhealthy to put yourself last? Explain.

4. We can assume that Jesus' principles of leadership, as explained in Matthew 23:11-12, are true for spiritual leadership. Do you think that they also apply to secular positions and corporations?

5. What benefits can you see if someone who is spiritually gifted for a spotlight position, such as teaching, also took time to serve in church cleaning or working in the nursery?

6. What can a person who receives frequent praise do to

maintain a servant heart?

7. Is a sensitive spirit more of a personality trait, a spiritual gift, or something that anyone can develop? Explain.

8. Eims believes that one thing a leader must do above all else is to get to know the people as individuals. How can a leader of a large group possibly accomplish this?

9. Read several different versions of 1 Thessalonians 5:14. Which group listed is the most difficult for you to work with? The easiest? Why?

10. What ideas have you seen (or can you imagine) that encourage caring for people as individuals with different needs?

11. How might a leader's attitude toward others influence the group he or she leads?

Prayer Focus

* Thank the Lord for the example of Jesus as a sensitive servant/leader. Pray that God will enable you to become more like Christ.

Optional Activities

1. Look up twenty or thirty references in the Bible of serve, servant, and service. Notice the insights that come from the different passages. Try to go through one whole day of ONLY serving others and putting yourself last in every circumstance.

2. In your own area of leadership, implement one concrete change to display more of a servant attitude or a sensitive spirit. Share this with someone who can pray for you.

Assignment

1. Read chapter 5 of the text and work through the study.

2. Take a self-inventory of your ministry and see which areas you excel in and which areas you need to work on. In those that you excel in, what makes the difference?

F i v e

Why Some Leaders Excel

Session Topic

To be leaders who excel, we must ask the Lord for a sense of excellence, initiative, and creativity.

Community Builder

1. Choose a public leader who is well known to those in your group. Discuss what qualities make him or her stand out.

2. Pretend that you are a student leader on a youth group camping trip. How might you show the traits of excellence, initiative, and creativity?

Discovery Questions

1. When you think of the title "Why Some Leaders Excel," what qualities or accomplishments come to mind?

2. On page 53, Eims states that if you do something in the name of the Lord, it should "reflect well on that name" and be "exceedingly magnificent." He also calls a sloppily done church bulletin "a scandal and a disgrace." What is your opinion about the necessity of excellence in Christian ministry?

3. Review the seven ways to bring about the spirit of excellence mentioned on page 55. Which of these, if any, has been most effective in your life as a means of moving you toward excellence?

4. On page 57, Eims describes Jesus Christ as "the only one who has ever done all things well, every moment of every hour of every day of His life." Do you believe that Jesus must have done ALL things well, even such things as cooking fish or combing His hair? Explain.

5. In what practical ways can we "completely relax in the arms of Jesus" as Eims advises on page 57?

6. If we are to attain a Christlike standard of excellence, where does our own effort fit in?

7. How does Eims define initiative? In what ways is initiative a Godlike characteristic?

8. Name the three ways that Eims suggests to exercise initiative. What other ways might you add?

9. What sets a godly leader's initiative apart from a nonbelieving leader's initiative?

10. What are some things you can do to gain a creative spirit?

11. As we try to be creative, how can we retain what is valuable in traditional methods and goals?

12. Do you think that it is acceptable for a Christian to decide "I want to be a leader that excels" and to work toward it? Explain.

13. What would happen if a leader took the three characteristics (excellence, initiative, and creativity) too far?

14. How can we know if we are excelling in our ministry?

Prayer Focus
* Pray for your leaders and for yourself to develop excellence, initiative, and creativity for God's glory. Thank the Lord for His work through you.

Optional Activities
1. Choose one area of your ministry or work and check to see how you are doing in terms of excellence, initiative, and creativity.

2. Peruse Christian media this week, looking for examples of excellence, initiative, and creativity.

Assignment
1. Read chapter 6 of the text and work through the study.

2. Decide on the specific impact you would like to make in your ministry.

Six

How to Make an Impact

Session Topic
In order to make an impact as a leader, a person must be wholehearted, single-minded, and have a fighting spirit.

Community Builder
1. If you could choose one area of ministry to focus on for the rest of your life, what would you choose? Be as specific as possible.

2. Are you usually very focused on one thing at a time or are you a jack-of-all-trades? What are the pros and cons of this?

Discovery Questions
1. Are you basically an optimist or a pessimist when it comes to making major changes or having a big impact on your world?

2. In view of your general attitude about change, what do you think about Hezekiah's story that Eims relates on page 66?

3. Do you think most people you know need to hear "take it easy"? Could you say that you are eager and zealous?

4. On page 67, Eims says that God wants people who are eager and zealous. Explain.

5. If a pastor were married and had young children, what would a wholehearted, zealous commitment to the Lord look like in a weekly schedule?

6. Eims speaks of Bible passages that refer to being "consumed with zeal for God" (p. 70). Why is this so rare in our own experience?

7. How do you feel around someone who is "on fire" for the Lord?

8. What are some ways that a person might decide which area of service to singlemindedly zero in on and stick with?

9. Do you consider it single-minded to serve as a church lay leader while working a 9-to-5 secular job? Explain.

10. Focus on Hebrews 12:1-2. What kinds of sins do you think most commonly entangle Christian leaders in their "race"?

11. What weights or encumbrances hold us back?

12. Name the three ways Eims believes a person can destroy his or her own life (see page 73). Which one are you most prone to? How do you press on when you feel this resistance?

13. In 2 Timothy 2:3, the Apostle Paul exhorts us to "endure hardship." In our culture, what hardships might a Christian leader be called upon to suffer for Christ's sake?

14. How can a "fighting spirit" fit in with other Christian qualities such as peace, gentleness, and kindness?

15. How can leaders who want to make an impact for the Lord increase their characteristics of being wholehearted, single-minded, and having a fighting spirit?

Prayer Focus

* Pray about the three areas Eims speaks about in this chapter. Confess where you've fallen short, give thanks for where you are doing well, and ask what God might want you to change in order to have more impact for His kingdom.

Optional Activities

1. Read a biography of someone famous in church history. Note how the three areas were present (or not present) throughout that person's life.

2. Notice someone else making an impact for God and affirm him or her in one of the three areas.

Assignment

1. Read chapter 7 and work through the study.

2. Consider how you have thus far set the stage for success in your work or ministry.

S e v e n

Setting the Stage for Success

Session Topic
Three things that set the stage for success as a ministry leader are: getting off to a good start, doing your homework, and planning the work.

Community Builder
1. Your real-life task, if you should choose to accept it, is to work together to show appreciation in some way (for example, to a pastor, secretary, host/hostess of meeting). Discuss who, when, how, and so on. When you are finished, evaluate the process by considering Eims' 4-step POLE plan (on p. 85).

2. Discuss the term "success" in relation to ministry. If you had to evaluate a ministry's success, what would you look for?

Discovery Questions
1. Why is it so important to plan a good beginning to a ministry? What characterizes a good beginning?

2. What should a leader do if he or she gets started on the wrong foot?

3. On page 81, Eims retells a biblical story about Saul. When have you, like Saul, tried to avoid leadership by hiding "among the baggage"?

4. Eims states on page 82 that after being chosen to lead, "don't be in a hurry to make a lot of changes." If you stepped in as a leader into a floundering ministry, how would you decide when to be patient and when to act?

5. What strikes you most about the story of Nehemiah as summarized on pages 83-84?

6. When have you ever missed an opportunity because you were not prepared? Or conversely, when were you able to

make good use of an opportunity because you were prepared?

7. Of the four steps in the POLE (Plan, Organize, Lead, and Evaluate), which are you the strongest in? Which are you the weakest in? Describe when you showed that strength or weakness.

8. What are you looking for when you select key people to work with you in your area of ministry?

9. How can you evaluate whether a person is capable before giving him or her a key task?

10. If you are seeing no development of Christlikeness in those whom you are responsible for, what might that mean? What can you do?

Prayer Focus

* Thank the Lord for your opportunity to serve by leading. Pray that He will help you plan for and measure success by godly standards. Have a time of silent prayer for your specific needs as a leader.

Optional Activities

1. Review Paul's prayers and how he prayed for the people he was leading. Pray over and seek specific ways to encourage Christlikeness in others in your ministry.

2. On your next leadership project, try the POLE system, and write down how you did each step and the results. Share this with someone in your study group.

Assignment

1. Read chapter 8 of the text and work through the study.

2. Consider how you feel about the amount of work you have compared to the amount of time you have. What Christian and secular books or ideas have influenced you in this regard?

Eight

How to Get More Done

Session Topic

Remember three things when you want to get more done: get right at it, trust God for the help you need, and focus on objectives instead of obstacles.

Community Builder

1. Make a list of everything you would have liked to get done today—if there were no obstacles.

2. Draw on a big sheet of paper pictures of things you need to do and the obstacles before you. Have other group members guess what you are drawing. After a correct guess, brainstorm ways God might overcome each obstacle. (For example, draw a Bible to signify devotions, and then draw a person sleeping.)

Discovery Questions

1. What were your first thoughts when you saw the title "How to Get More Done"?

2. Review the story of Moses as related on pages 89-90. Imagine your reaction to God's command to count the congregation. What might make that situation different than your assignments today?

3. Read aloud Matthew 11:28-30. How does this speak to you as a busy, maybe burdened, Christian leader?

4. Eims' first suggestion is to "do it now." In what circumstances would this be the right thing to do? Are there times when it wouldn't be right?

5. In the booklet, *Tyranny of the Urgent,* the author gives the opposite advice. He says the urgent things usually aren't the important things and they must wait or the important things will be squeezed out. How do you balance this with

Eims' advice to "do it now"?

6. Can you recall an incident in which God provided the help you needed when you faced an overwhelming task?

7. Do you think we should see some obstacles as God saying "stop"? If so, how would you know in which instances to stop and when to press on in faith?

8. In our trusting that God will provide help, and the right kind of help, where does recruiting efforts on our own part fit in?

9. Do you seem to be "wired to think negatively"? If so, how does this usually show up in your life? If not, to what do you attribute your positive thinking?

10. What can you do to (1) notice when you are being problem-centered and (2) change that to being goal-centered?

Optional Activities

1. Read Ephesians 5:15-16; Luke 18:27; and other verses that encourage your faith in accomplishing God's work.

2. Consider how Jesus managed His time. What did He spend most of his time doing? For further thought on this, read *The Master Plan of Evangelism* by Robert E. Coleman.

Prayer Focus

* Thank the Lord for the many days you've already had to love and serve Him. Pray that you will use each day for His glory. Ask for wisdom in your daily decisions and responses. Lift up one specific decision or obstacle to Him.

Assignment

1. Read chapter 9 and work through the study.

2. Take stock of recent or present difficulties to determine where the problem lies and how you are handling it.

Nine

Resolving Difficulties

Session Topic
Four principles are helpful when facing difficulties: (1) carefully select coleaders, (2) keep the lines of communication open, (3) keep a well-balanced program, and (4) face the difficulties of life in light of the cross of Christ.

Community Builders
1. Have Rubik's Cubes or other difficult puzzles for group members to try upon arrival. How do different people approach the resolution of this difficulty?
2. Test juggling skills of group members bit by bit to illustrate that one must be able or faithful to do the little things before they can do it all. Can they toss one tennis ball up and down? If not, forget it! Give them two balls and see if they can throw up one after the other in rhythm. If anyone can do two balls, add a third. Discuss.

Discovery Questions
1. As you began your work or ministry, what was your reaction when the first problems surfaced? Are problems in your work mostly problems with the group or problems in your personal life?
2. In your ministry, what role does the Word of God play? How do you follow Eims' example to "help people learn what the Bible says and help them apply its truths to their everyday situations" (p. 103)?
3. Discuss Dawson Trotman's statement on page 103: "Telling is not teaching; listening is not learning." In what way could you apply this in your leadership?
4. What has been your experience, as a leader, with dele-

gation? Are there any signs or signals that tell you it is time to delegate?

5. List the three qualities Eims lists for choosing coworkers. Would you add any other qualities to that list? What quality do you most want?

6. Eims advises on page 105 that there be "agreement on goals; much latitude in method and means." Do you agree? How difficult is it for you to relinquish control of the method and means?

7. How did the smaller previous responsibilities you had before your present leadership role prepare you?

8. Why is good communication with coworkers so difficult?

9. What unpleasant tasks do you find yourself avoiding? How do you counteract this?

10. When adversity comes, some people become bitter at God while others draw nearer to God. What makes the difference?

11. Can you recall a time when giving a burden or difficulty to the Lord lightened your load?

Prayer Focus

* Praise the Lord for His loving care for us to deliver us out of and through difficulties. Pray about one specific difficulty, and then practice giving it over to the Lord.

Optional Activities

1. Search the Scriptures to learn even more about resolving difficulties. You may want to look in a concordance under the words: problem, difficulty, trial, or conflict.

2. Consider how this chapter might also apply to family relationships as you seek to prevent or resolve difficulties there.

Assignment

1. Read chapter 10 and work through the study.

2. Discuss with another leader or coworker the greatest dangers of your position.

T e n

Surviving Dangers

Session Topic

If we trust God, He can and will deliver us from the three things that can be the downfall of a leader: a covetous heart, a craving for self-glory, and discouragement.

Community Builders

1. Brainstorm together to think of your favorite games (for example, Monopoly, Nintendo) and the dangers you must survive to win. Then try to name and even create a game where the dangers would be spiritually deadly like the three in this chapter.

2. List and rank in order what you believe are the top five dangers that a Christian leader faces in your type of ministry. Discuss.

Discovery Questions

1. What sorts of dangers have you seen most often hinder or destroy a Christian leader?

2. What are the three deadliest dangers to a leader, according to Eims, and how would you summarize each one?

3. In Philippians 3:17-19, who are these "enemies of the cross"? Rephrase in your own words the four descriptions of those people.

4. What words come to your mind as synonyms for "covetousness"? Read aloud Colossians 3:1-5. What does this passage say to do about these desires? How would one do that?

5. What are the two reasons Eims gives for why covetousness is so deadly? (See pp. 120-121.)

6. If a person were free from covetousness, what would characterize that person? Describe what you think is a proper

view of money and possessions?

7. Why is self-glory, or pride, so subtle?

8. As a leader who might someday receive honor and prestige, how can you properly handle the spotlight, the extra attention, the special invitations?

9. Of the three areas Eims lists (giving, production for the Lord, and service for Christ), which draws you most toward self-glory? Explain.

10. Of the four lessons about discouragement that Eims draws from the Elijah story on pages 128-129, which speaks to you most strongly? Why? How does David's story differ (pp. 129-130)?

11. What is the one personal application you can take home concerning surviving dangers in your work or ministry?

Prayer Focus

* Thank the Lord for clear warnings in Scripture, and confess any sins or failings in these danger areas. Pray for strength and protection from both the subtle and obvious dangers to your ministry.

Optional Activities

1. Memorize one or more of God's promises that you can hold onto when faced with the discussed dangers to your ministry. Some suggestions are Philippians 1:6, 4:11-13; 1 Corinthians 10:13; 2 Corinthians 3:4-6; 12:9-10; Hebrews 13:5-6.

2. Choose one danger to which you feel especially vulnerable. Ask a fellow believer to pray for you. Draw up a spiritual battle plan to ward off attacks in this area.

Assignment

1. Read chapter 11 and work through the study.

2. Recall people you have previously ministered to and consider how well you have led them to become Christ's disciples.

Eleven
Meeting the Needs of the Group

Session Topic
The best way to meet the needs of the group you lead is by deepening their spiritual lives through discipleship and training.

Community Builders
1. Here is an advanced exercise in mathematics. Let's say Susan led Grace to Christ and discipled her for one year. At the end of that year, Susan discipled Brittanny while Grace discipled Joy. The third year, Susan, Grace, Joy, and Brittany each discipled a new person and the chain continued. At the end of three years, how many discipling Christians would there be? How about five or ten years? (Hint: Draw a diagram.)

2. What are your dreams for your current work and for your lifelong work or ministry? What goals would help you fulfill those dreams?

Discovery Questions
1. How would you feel if the Lord called you as a pastor over a church of 400 people like those described in 1 Samuel 22:2?

2. How do you react to the principle of leadership: "It takes one to make one"? (Encouraged? Frightened? Challenged? Other?) Why?

3. What signs would you look for to see if a person is ready to make disciples one-on-one? What signs would show that a person is ready to make disciples in a group setting?

4. Review pages 133-140. What is Eims' suggested two-point program to help each person develop to the maximum? What modifications, if any, would you need to make in order to use this plan in your own setting?

5. How do you feel about early morning meetings? Have you ever participated in or led one? Describe how it went — or how you think it would go.

6. How could you begin if you don't detect a special interest in anyone? What might be the reason for this?

7. Of the verses and goals listed on pages 134-136, which do you think would be most appealing for your group?

8. Which Bible study programs or booklets have you found to work out the best? Why do you think these worked well?

9. What are your thoughts on embarking on a discipleship program where you train a group or work one-on-one? How can you, as leaders, help one another get going and stay going?

10. Did you have anyone who discipled you? If so, what were the benefits? If not, what difference do you think it would have made?

11. Read 2 Timothy 2:2. Do you think that this pattern works with any age? Is it different with men than women? Could it work parent to child? Explain.

Prayer Focus

* Thank God for being in this study group, redeemed and growing in faith, instead of fallen away or lost. Ask the Lord to enlarge your life for His glory and to make your leadership productive even beyond your wildest dreams.

Optional Activities

1. Prayerfully evaluate the focus and goals of your work, and how the making of disciples needs to be added or enhanced.

2. Ask around to see if many in your church or fellowship group have ever been discipled, if they wish they had been or could be, or if they would like to disciple someone else. If appropriate, report your findings to someone who might be able to meet those needs — or become that organizer yourself!

Assignment

1. Read chapter 12 and work through the study.

2. Notice this week the different methods and styles your various leaders use to communicate with you.

Twelve

Communication

Session Topic
In order to communicate effectively, you must know what you are talking about and you must mean what you say.

Community Builders
1. Describe the best sermon, talk, or lecture you remember, and explain why it was so memorable.
2. Tell a story about your own experiences as an up-front communicator.

Discovery Questions
1. What role does communication play in your current ministry? What do you foresee as issues about communication in your future ministry?
2. Review Eims' two imperatives in speaking on page 142. Which is the easiest for you to excel in and why?
3. Of the preachers and religious services currently on TV, whose communication style do you like the best? What do you like about it? What really turns you off? (If you don't watch TV preachers, explain why.)
4. Review the pattern for the content of a message as Eims presents it on pages 144-145. Would you change or add anything?
5. Where can you find stories or illustrations? How can you keep from using the same ones over and over?
6. What signs of nervousness do you get before speaking? Which is easier for you, communicating one-on-one, to a group, or to an audience? What verses or techniques help with your nervousness?
7. What things do you pray about when you are to present a message? Do you consider praying a strength for you or a

weak point?

8. How can you be reminded or motivated to pray more concerning your communication opportunities?

9. Which chapter of this book was most helpful to you? Why?

10. Which principles or ideas have stuck with you as you've gone through this study?

11. What has been the most challenging area for you?

12. What changes have you made (or will you make) in your leadership as a result of this study?

Prayer Focus

* Thank the Lord for the communication opportunities you have, and ask Him to show you how to be more effective for His sake. Pray for the whole group to become more and more the leaders God wants you to be. Pray for the person on your right (or some other designation) in his or her specific ministry opportunities.

Optional Activities

1. Ask a trusted believer to attend when you are presenting a message or communicating in some way. Videotape it if possible. Then ask for feedback and discuss your presentation. (Be sure you really are open to hearing it before you do this.) Work on making changes toward more effective communication.

2. As you listen to various speakers in different situations, observe their content and manner of presentation. If you have a tendency toward becoming critical, ask the Lord for a generous spirit as you observe. See what you can learn from others.

Assignment

Go in the strength and the power of the Lord . . . and *Be the Leader You Were Meant to Be!*